THE EMPOWERED PARALEGAL

THE EMPOWERED PARALEGAL

EFFECTIVE, EFFICIENT AND PROFESSIONAL

ROBERT E. MONGUE
ASSISTANT PROFESSOR OF LEGAL STUDIES
UNIVERSITY OF MISSISSIPPI

CAROLINA ACADEMIC PRESS
Durham, North Carolina

Library of Congress Cataloging-in-Publication Data

Mongue, Robert E.
  The empowered paralegal : effective, efficient and professional / Robert E.
Mongue.
      p. cm.
  Includes index.
  ISBN 978-1-59460-685-4 (alk. paper)
  1. Legal assistants--United States--Handbooks, manuals, etc. 2. Legal assis-
tants--Vocational guidance--United States. I. Title.

  KF320.L4M66 2009
  340.023'73--dc22

                                        2009018862

CAROLINA ACADEMIC PRESS
700 Kent Street
Durham, North Carolina 27701
Telephone (919) 489-7486
Fax (919) 493-5668
www.cap-press.com

Printed in the United States of America

To Denise, without whom this book and most everything else would not have been possible, and (in alphabetical order) to Caroline, Ethan, Justin, Patrick and Tyler.

CONTENTS

INTRODUCTION

The Paralegal — An Essential Part of the Legal Team

Paralegals are more skilled, more professional and better educated than ever. As a result they are taking on more and more of the tasks formerly handled by attorneys.

The profession itself is rapidly growing. According to the United States Bureau of Labor Statistics, it is one of the fastest growing occupations in America, with an expected increase in positions of twenty-two percent between 2006 and 2016, much faster than average for all other occupations.[1] There are literally hundreds of training programs available for paralegals, ranging from certificate programs to full bachelor degrees. Many of these have obtained voluntary approval from the American Bar Association. Some states are considering licensing or certification requirements. Both the National Association of Legal Assistants (NALA) and National Federation of Paralegal Associations (NFPA) offer certifications.

Yet, every workday thousands of paralegals and legal assistants leave their office feeling frustrated, overworked and under utilized. Much of this dissatisfaction flows from lack of paralegal empowerment and lack of understanding of the roles played by each member of the legal team. Let's take a look at how we would like it to be.

A. An Empowered Paralegal

The Smiths sit on packing crates in the disarray that is their new home. They smile as they toast each other and their new purchase, reflecting on

---

1. United States Department of Labor, Bureau of Labor Statistics, http://www.bls.gov/oco/ocos114.htm (Accessed February 26, 2009).

how smoothly the closing, in fact the entire purchase process, went ear-
lier that day. As they contemplate unpacking, they are confident and se-
cure in their new ownership because they know the deed and other
paperwork were correctly done; the title thoroughly examined and the
title insurance in place. Each step of the way they were part of the process,
fully informed and impressed by the competence of John, their attorney's
paralegal.

At each stage of the process, from their decision to sell their old home to
the closing, John made them part of the legal team. Their initial contact
with Attorney Morgan's office began with their interview with John, who was
able to quickly obtain the information necessary for Anita Morgan to com-
plete all the steps necessary to protect them legally. From the start, John ex-
plained the process in terms they could understand, including the likely time
sequence. As the purchase and sale process progressed, the Smiths were con-
fident that John understood their case and was keeping track of deadlines.
Of course, John was careful not to give legal advice. It was clear to the Smiths
where John's responsibilities ended and Anita's began. John's competence
increased their confidence in Anita. They appreciated the efficiency of
their meetings with Anita even though they did not know the extent to
which Anita's application of her extensive legal knowledge to their case
depended on John's interaction with them and with Anita.

The Smiths' closing would no doubt have occurred even if John were not as
an effective paralegal as he was, but they are satisfied with their legal experience
because they, John and Attorney Morgan all understood his vital role as a paralegal in Anita's office. John's role goes well beyond his knowledge of the law and
legal ethics learned during his paralegal studies. John has acquired the ability to
apply that knowledge as part of the legal team in a practical law office setting.

In addition to his legal knowledge, John has learned the essential skills of
an effective, empowered paralegal:

- The effective, empowered paralegal manages time well. Generally, a lawyer
  sells legal services, rather than a product. The value of those services is
  measured by the amount of time spent fulfilling a client's legal needs. It
  is essential, therefore, that both the paralegal and the attorney organize
  themselves and their time to maximize efficiency. In addition, they must
  keep track of, and bill for, their time in a way that makes sense for the
  law office and the clients.
- The effective, empowered paralegal manages the calendar well. Missed deadlines result in dissatisfied clients, malpractice claims, and attorney disciplinary procedures. It is essential that both the attorney and the paralegal

be aware of upcoming deadlines and have a system in place to meet those
deadlines without last-minute pressures that increase the likelihood of
mistakes.

- The effective, empowered paralegal manages files well. The best crafted deeds, contracts, wills and pleadings are worthless if they cannot be found when needed. None of them can even be created if the necessary information cannot be located in a timely manner, or was never obtained in the first place. It is essential that both the paralegal and the attorney have a system in place and use that system for organizing, identifying, indexing and tracking files and the materials contained in the files.
- The effective, empowered paralegal manages clients well. The client is part of the legal team. Without the client there is no need for either the paralegal or the attorney and there is no money to fund the law office. However, the client is the member of the team who knows least about the law and her role in the team. It is essential that the paralegal and the attorney keep the client informed about what is being done for her, why it is being done and what she needs to do for the outcome to be successful.
- The effective, empowered paralegal manages the paralegal's relationship with the attorney well within the legal team. Both the paralegal and attorney must know and respect their roles and those of the other, their abilities and those of the other. It is essential that the paralegal understand what the attorney expects of him and the attorney understand what the paralegal can and cannot do for her.
- The effective, empowered paralegal knows and applies the principles of professionalism and thereby gains recognition of his status as a professional.

During thirty years as a litigator employing, training and teaching paralegals, I have gathered and developed clear, concise and easy-to-use techniques for empowering paralegals as a critical component of the effective legal team. I have used these techniques in my own law practice, in classrooms, seminars and workshops.

These techniques are now set out and explained in this practical guide to becoming *The Empowered Paralegal*. Each of the essential skills is examined in more detail, with management of time, workload, docket, files, clients and attorneys each being the focus of their own chapter. Professionalism must be part of every aspect of the paralegal's performance, so it will be part of each chapter and discussed extensively in the chapters on managing clients and managing attorneys. In addition, we will discuss the role of the paralegal, the attorney and the client in each of the areas and offer practical approaches to dealing with the issues that arise in a law practice. We will also examine some potential ethical issues and malpractice pitfalls.

In Chapter Seven, we'll bring the Five Essential Skills together in the context of managing a litigation file using Crucial Tools for Building a Better Trial. Finally, we will discuss briefly how each of the skills and tools can be used by paralegals in any type of law practice.

B. Understanding the Legal Team

Our discussion has to start with an understanding of who the members of the legal team are and the role each member plays in relation to the legal matter being handled by the team. A diagram of the traditional concept of the legal team looks much like a corporation or government organizational chart with a rigid hierarchy of commands, responsibilities and duties.

Figure 1

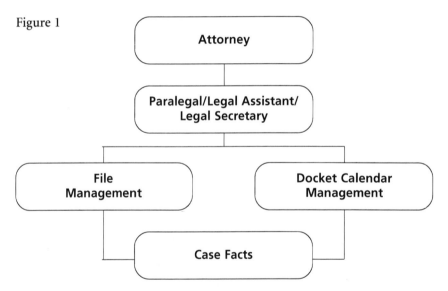

This traditional view of the legal team suffers from several flaws, the most prominent of which is that if fails to recognize any role for the client. Every law office gives some importance to the client in the sense they acknowledge that without the client there is no case and no fee. This type of recognition results in only a minor change to the chart, as shown in Figure 2.

However, recognizing this importance of the client to the law office is not the same as recognizing the client as part of the legal team; rather it keeps the client apart from the team and, to a great extent, from the very legal matter which brought the client to the attorney.

Figure 2

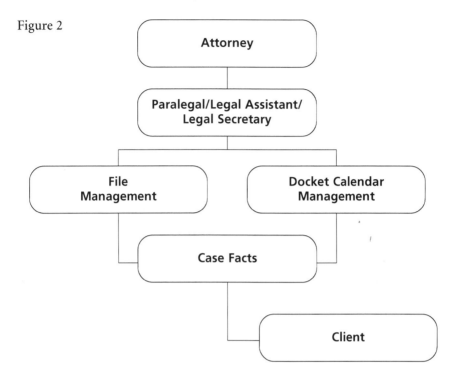

We will discuss the role of the client in depth in Chapter Five. The roles of the paralegal and the attorney will be discussed throughout this book and are the focus of Chapter Six. For now, it is necessary only that we be aware that in this book the client, the paralegal and the attorney are all members of the legal team. This conception of the roles of each member in the legal team differs from the traditional view. The conception used in this book is better in the following diagram (Figure 3) than the traditional diagram.

This diagram begins to account for these fundamental *inter*relationships and responsibilities:

- The interrelationship between the facts, the file, the docket and time;
- The interrelationship between the client, the paralegal and the attorney; and
- The joint responsibility and involvement of all members of the legal team for the facts, the file and the docket in achieving a successful outcome.

These interrelationships and responsibilities appear more complex than they have often been characterized and will be discussed extensively in this book. The goal for the effective, empowered paralegal is the ability to understand and to

Figure 3

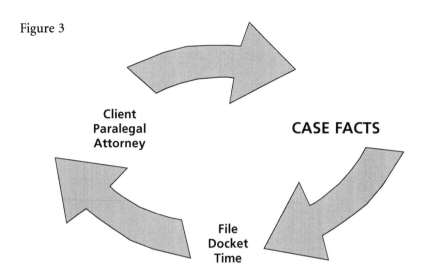

Client
Paralegal
Attorney

CASE FACTS

File
Docket
Time

manage each of the key factors. It's simpler than it sounds. We'll start in Chapter One by learning to manage your time.

THE EMPOWERED
PARALEGAL

Chapter One

Managing Your Time— Yes, Time Is Money!

Time is the mainstay and main product of a law office. The importance of time management rests not only in its monetary value. Managing your time and helping your attorney manage time not only increases productivity and efficiency, but also increases accuracy and job satisfaction. It also reduces ethical and malpractice complaints. However, many people do not have a clear understanding of what it means to manage time. Take Susan for example:

> *Susan arrived twenty minutes late for lunch with John. She apologized profusely while simultaneously sliding papers into her portfolio and reaching for her cell phone, which could be heard buzzing over the din of the deli. She again smiled apologetically to John, indicating it was her attorney on the phone. When she finally sat down and flipped the cell phone shut she sighed deeply, but took a moment to make a note in her Palm Pilot.*
> *Others in the deli watched her performance with admiration. She appeared to be the model of multi-tasking efficiency. A few glanced knowingly at John, who sat patiently reviewing the newspaper. They and he knew that in fact Susan simply didn't know how to manage her time.*

The paralegal who can arrive for lunch dates on time knowing he has correctly and successfully completed the morning's work and thus can enjoy the lunch, approaches the afternoon with an entirely different attitude than the paralegal who is constantly overwhelmed by work.

The effective, empowered paralegal knows how to organize, protect and track time, making time theirs rather than belonging to the time demands of the job.[1] Let's take a look at some of techniques useful in managing time.

---

1. This is true of any profession and occupation. As a result, there are many guides, workshops and consultants who deal with the management of time. I have benefited from several of these experts during the course of my career. I am particularly indebted for purposes of this work by the teachings of Frank Sanitate, author of *Don't Go To Work Unless*

A. Organizing Yourself and Your Time

The first step in time organization is organizing yourself, your workspace and your work. Let's start with the last and work backwards.

First, we need to know what your work is. Of course, in general, the paralegal's work is to assist an attorney, or in some cases, several attorneys. However, each paralegal's work will vary depending on the work normally handled by that paralegal's attorney, the structure of the office in which the paralegal works, and the division of responsibilities between the attorney, the paralegal, other law office staff, outside contractors and the client.

The identification and division of responsibilities amongst the attorney, paralegal and client will be discussed more extensively in later chapters. It may be necessary for you and your attorney to have a better understanding regarding this division. In the meantime, let's take a look at your present situation.

Prepare a Job Description

Now I sound like an attorney. We are talking about managing time and the first thing I want you to do is add a "To Do" item to your task list. I'll be doing this a lot throughout this book, but with good reason. I'm sure you have heard the adage, "It takes money to make money." It is equally true that it will take time to manage time. It will be worth it in the end! Spend the time wisely now and you'll have it back three-fold later. And a bit later, we will ask your attorney to help by preparing an attorney's version of your job description so we can compare the two.

Don't go looking for the job description you were given during your employment orientation. Even if you can find it, it is not likely to describe your work the way we need it described. Even if it is an accurate description of the office's conception of your job, it is important that we have an accurate description of *your job the way it is done by you.*

Start by making a list of each of the tasks required by your job in the order in which they occur to you. State the tasks in their simplest form. Do you open the mail and read the mail? List the task as "Open the mail and read mail." Does the secretary open the mail and leave it for your to read? List the task as "Read the Mail" After reading the mail, what do you do with it? Sort it? File it? Answer it? You may not need a separate line for each part of the task, but make

---

It's Fun! State-Of-The-Heart Time Management. More information about Mr. Sanitate is available at http://www.franksanitate.com.

sure you list each part. What else? Call clients, take client calls, draft pleadings, prepare exhibits, conduct legal research, contact title abstractors, contact investigators, contact guardians-ad-litem? Only you know what is *really* required to do your job. When the list is complete, you likely will be surprised at what your job entails; your attorney almost certainly will be surprised. Even so, leave plenty of space to add tasks later as you think of them.

Now that we can stand back and see what you do as a paralegal, it's easy to see why it seems overwhelming at times. There are so many demands on your time, it is a wonder *anything* ever gets done, but it does and *you do it*. More importantly, now that we can stand back and see what you do as a paralegal, we can begin to organize the tasks and the time so that the tasks are accomplished in a way that makes sense—the most important tasks take priority over others, daily tasks are done daily, weekly tasks are done weekly, and so on. All we need to do is figure out which tasks are which and how they are best organized in the time *you* have to do them.

Prioritize Your Tasks

We need to know more than just what you do to manage your time. We also need to know how often you do each task, how long each task takes, and how important each task is in relation to the other tasks on the list.

Start by making five columns on a sheet of paper. Label the columns "Task," "Frequency," "Time," "Priority" and "Who/What Else." It is helpful to go to your word processor's "Page Setup" function and turn your paper to the "Landscape" setting for this:

Figure 1.1: Chart for Prioritizing Tasks

Task	Frequency	Time	Priority	Who/What Else

Enter your tasks in the "Task" column and then we'll focus on the next three columns.

Figure 1.2: Chart with Task Column Completed

Task	Frequency	Time	Priority	Who/ What Else
Open and sort mail				
Call clients				
Post to file				
Draft pleadings				
File Corporate Annual Reports				
File IRS Form 941				
Order medical records				
Follow up on medical record orders				
Review and sort medical records				
Send medical records to adjuster				

In the "Frequency" column list how often the task must be performed—daily, weekly, monthly, quarterly or annually. The frequency with which you perform some tasks will vary depending on season, work load and the like. It will be necessary to review and revise your overall time management plan accordingly, but for now enter the current frequency.

Figure 1.3: Chart with Frequency Column Completed

Task	Frequency	Time	Priority	Who/ What Else
Open and sort mail	Daily			
Call clients	Daily			
Post to file	Daily			
Draft pleadings	Weekly			
File Corporate Annual Reports	Annually			
File IRS Form 941	Quarterly			
Order medical records	Weekly			
Follow up on medical record orders	Monthly			
Review and sort medical records	Weekly			
Send medical records to adjuster	Weekly			

In the "Time" column list the usual amount of time required to complete the task. State the time in tenths of an hour, i.e., twelve minutes equals .2 hours. Round up to the nearest tenth—chances are your attorney does. (Figure 1.4)

In the "Priority" column list the relative priority of that item in relation to other items done with the same frequency. For example, if you must generally

Figure 1.4: Chart with Priority Column Completed

Task	Frequency	Time	Priority	Who/ What Else
Open and sort mail	Daily	.7 hrs		
Call clients	Daily	.8		
Post to file	Daily	.8		
Draft pleadings	Weekly	2.0		
File Corporate Annual Reports	Annually	10.0		
File IRS Form 941	Quarterly	6.5		
Order medical records	Weekly	1.8		
Follow up on medical record orders	Monthly	1.0		
Review and sort medical records	Weekly	3.5		
Send medical records to adjuster	Weekly	1.6		

open, read and sort mail every day and call clients every day, which of those tasks is more important? One way to judge this is by asking which one could best be put off until the next day if it were absolutely necessary to put one off. Failure to open mail may result in delay in responding. Failure to call back a client will violate a policy of returning all calls within twenty-four hours. Neither is desirable, but one is less desirable than the other; that one has higher priority.

Figure 1.5: Chart with Priority Column Completed

Task	Frequency	Time	Priority	Who/ What Else
Open and sort mail	Daily	.7 hrs	1	
Call clients	Daily	.8	2	
Post to file	Daily	.8	3	
Draft pleadings	Weekly	2.0	2	
File Corporate Annual Reports	Annually	10.0	1	
File IRS Form 941	Quarterly	6.5	1	
Order medical records	Weekly	1.8	3	
Follow up on medical record orders	Monthly	1.0	4	
Review and sort medical records	Weekly	3.5	2	
Send medical records to adjuster	Weekly	1.6	3	

Grouping

We now know what your job requires each day, week, month, quarter and year, how much time must be allocated to each and how important each is. If we group all the daily items together or highlight them in their own color and do the same with weekly, monthly, quarterly and yearly items, we can organize your day, week and so on, in a way that allows you to control your time while accomplishing your work.

Figure 1.6: Chart with Tasks Grouped by Frequency

Task	Frequency	Time	Priority	Who/ What Else
Open and sort mail	Daily	.7 hrs	1	
Call clients	Daily	.8	2	
Post to file	Daily	.8	3	
Draft pleadings	Weekly	2.0	2	
Review and sort medical records	Weekly	3.5	2	
Order medical records	Weekly	1.8	3	
Follow up on medical record orders	Monthly	1.0	4	
File IRS Form 941	Quarterly	6.5	1	
File Corporate Annual Reports	Annually	10.0	1	

Solutions to Time Overload

It just might be that when we add up all the time required to do your daily or weekly tasks, the total time is more than you have in your work day or week. This is not surprising. Nor is it as hopeless a situation as it may seem. There are solutions. We'll discuss the ones over which you have the most control a bit later in this chapter, for example, organizing yourself, organizing your work and workspace and protecting your time. Many of the others will require discussion with, and action by, your attorney. Chapter Six will discuss establishing communication with your attorney.

The best place to start is by eliminating tasks. Often a paralegal's job includes particular tasks because "we've always done it that way." The fact that the job has always included a certain task does not mean it must or even ought to be part of the job. As rules, procedures, policies and the like change, tasks are often added without much thought as to what task can be eliminated as a result of the changes. Start by reviewing the ten items with the lowest priority rankings on your Job Description Chart. With a little thought, it is likely that some of them can be removed from the list entirely. In the column labeled "Who/What Else" on your Job Description Chart, write "eliminate" for these items.

Next, consider who or what else can do tasks. Are you performing tasks that really should be performed by a legal secretary, an outside investigator, a filing clerk, your attorney, a machine or software? This is always a difficult issue, because everyone in the office is likely to feel as overloaded as you. It may be that the office needs to hire additional help, purchase equipment or upgrade software.

Figure 1.7: Chart with Possible Task Allocation Solutions

Task	Frequency	Time	Priority	Who/ What Else
Open and sort mail	Daily	.7 hrs	1	Mail Clerk
Call clients	Daily	.8	2	
Post to file	Daily	.8	3	File Clerk
Draft pleadings	Weekly	2.0	2	
Send medical records to adjuster	Weekly	1.6	3	Secretary
Review and sort medical records	Weekly	3.5	2	
Order medical records	Weekly	1.8	3	Secretary
Follow up on medical record orders	Monthly	1.0	4	Secretary
File IRS Form 941	Quarterly	6.5	1	Software?
File Corporate Annual Reports	Annually	10.0	1	

Additional expenditures are seldom any more welcome than suggestions that someone else take on additional tasks. However, if you really are overloaded, even after applying the principles and techniques discussed later in this book, then you are not likely to be able to do your full job well. In the long run, overloaded paralegals make mistakes or do incomplete work. This is generally more costly to a law office than the cost of the help needed to eliminate the overburden.

Also, it makes more financial sense to pay, for example, a filing clerk's pay rate for filing than to pay you to do it. If there is not enough of one type of work, say filing, to justify an additional staff person, perhaps it can be combined with other similar tasks such as opening and sorting mail. Frequently, simple tasks can be handled by a part-time worker, perhaps a student who works only a few hours a week after school.

For example, in the sample Job Description Chart you spend .7 hours a day (14 hours a month) opening and sorting mail, .8 hours a day (16 hours a month) filing documents, 1.8 hours a week (5.2 hours a month) ordering medical records, 1.6 hours a week (64 hours a month) sending those records to adjusters, and 1.0 hours a month doing medical record request follow-up, a total of 42.6 hours a month, about 10 hours a week or two hours a day.

Figure 1.8: Chart Illustrating Time Expenditures

Task	Frequency	Time	Weekly	Monthly
Open and sort mail	Daily	.7 hrs	3.5	14.0
Post to file	Daily	.8	4.0	16.0
Order medical records	Weekly	1.8	1.8	5.2
Follow up on medical record orders	Monthly	1.0		1.0
Send medical records to adjuster	Weekly	1.6	3	6.4
Total task performable by clerical staff				42.6 Hours

This is about 25% of your time spent on clerical work and detracting from more important tasks. It would make far more sense for you to be reviewing the medical records for content than ordering them from providers and mailing them to adjusters.

In addition, it doesn't make a lot of economic sense for your employer. The attorney is paying you paralegal rates for three-fourths of a paralegal's work. Let's say you are being paid $18 an hour, but could pay part-time clerical staff $8 an hour. The attorney is paying $200 for work that could be done for $89. The situation is worse if the attorney is paying for paralegal overtime!

Remember the real difficulty here is not the expense, but the fact that there are at least a full forty hours of paralegal work that needs to be done. This leaves you overwhelmed and perhaps frustrated. It means you cannot do your work thoroughly, and important work is being slighted for the sake of clerical tasks. The economic analysis is solely to illustrate that there is a solution that makes economic sense to the attorney.

Figure 1.9: Chart Showing Financial Benefit to the Office

Task	Weekly	$18.00/hr	$8.00/hr
Open and sort mail	3.5	63.00	28.00
Post to file	4.0	72.00	32.00
Order medical records	1.8	32.40	14.40
Follow up on medical record orders	.25	4.50	2.00
Send medical records to adjuster	1.6	28.80	12.80
Total task performable by clerical staff	11.15	$200.70	$89.20

Similarly, it may cost less to upgrade software or buy a piece of equipment than to pay you to do work better done another way. On the other hand, if the task really isn't worth additional costs, then there is a real question as to whether it needs to be done at all and should have been eliminated in step one.

Since you have been performing these tasks, you are in the best position to suggest alternatives. In fact, since you have been performing these tasks, it is unlikely anyone else has given much thought to alternatives. So take a few moments to think about each of the tasks on your list, starting with those of lowest priority. If you believe a task is best performed by someone or something else, indicate what you believe is the best alternative in the column labeled "Who/What Else" on your Job Description Chart. We'll come back to it later.

1 · MANAGING YOUR TIME

The First Priority

It is likely you have left a task off your list, a task that takes highest priority. Right now, add to your list of Daily Tasks "Organize and plan my day" and give it priority "1++." *Before* you check your voicemail, *before* you check your email, *before* you check notes from your attorney (but *after* you've made your coffee), plan out your day and the rest of your week. Looking at your Job Description Chart and knowing your files, you can see what must be done and what has priority.

Make a plan. Sure, plans change. You need to be flexible. Emergencies happen. Attorneys and clients change their minds. Priorities change. Your plan can and will change with them. You may need to plan twice; an initial plan that includes checking your voicemail, email and attorney notes and a second plan that incorporates new items or issues you found when you checked your voicemail, email and attorney. You may even plan for contingencies. But you can't manage your time if voicemails, emails, attorneys and clients are managing you. While I have often thought the word "proactive" should be banned from our language, you must be proactive rather than reactive when managing your time.

If you know you need to draft a Will for Mrs. Johnson and it will take an hour and a half, block off an hour and a half to do it. If it needs to be done today, then block it off today. If it is has to be done by Wednesday and it is only Monday, decide on which day it would be best to block off the time. Then schedule it on your calendar. Later we'll discuss how important it is to let other people know you need this time. For now, it is important that *you* know you need this time.

Chances are your week has a flow to it. Clients call most often on Monday mornings and Friday afternoons. The title abstractor always returns title work on Tuesdays. Your attorney is out of the office at hearings on Wednesday mornings. Use that knowledge to schedule your work in a convenient and efficient way. (See Figure 1.10.)

Figure 1.10: Chart Showing Planning Calendar

WEEK OF JANUARY 5, 2009

	Monday	Tuesday	Wednesday	Thursday	Friday
8:00	Make Daily & Weekly Plan	Make Daily Plan & Adjust Weekly Plan	Make Daily Plan & Adjust Weekly Plan	Make Daily Plan & Adjust Weekly Plan	Make Daily Plan, Begin Next Week's Plan
8:30	Mail & Voice Mail Review	Mail & Voice Mail Review	Mail & Voice Mail Review	Mail & Voice Mail Review	Mail & Voice Mail Review
9:00	Meet with Attorney— Coordinate Plans and	Finalize Jones Will—Arrange for witnesses		Draft Smith Discovery	
9:30	Responsibilities for week	–		Draft Smith Discovery	
10:00				Draft Smith Discovery	
10:30	Previously Scheduled				
11:00	Client Meeting		Confirm Witnesses for Jones Will Execution		
11:30	Lunch	Lunch	Lunch	Previously Scheduled Client Meeting	Lunch
12:00	Draft		With		
12:30	Johnson Will for		John		
1:00	attorney to review at 1:30			Lunch	
1:30	Meet with Attorney— Review Jones Will		Johnson Will Execution		
2:00		Previously Scheduled			
2:30		Client Meeting			
3:00	Return Calls	Return Calls	Return Calls	Return Calls	Return Calls
3:30	To Clients & Adjuster	To Clients & Adjuster	To Clients & Adjuster	To Clients & Adjuster	To Clients & Adjuster
4:00		Meet with Attorney— Prep for Wed. Hearings		Meet with Attorney— Review Smith Discovery Draft	
4:30					
5:00	Daily Filing	Daily Filing	Daily Filing	Daily Filing	Daily Filing

Now you have a Plan. There will be new demands and you will have to be flexible, but the new demands will be viewed in the context of your plan. When Attorney Horwitz rushes over and drops Clement Hodge's file on your desk with instructions to revise the codicil to Hodge's will "before noon," you will do it. But not before explaining to Attorney Horwitz that it will mean Mrs. Johnson's Will won't be ready at 1:30 as he had wanted. Together you will decide how best to prioritize these tasks and you can adjust your Plan accordingly. *You* will be managing your time.

Right now you are probably thinking, "This will never happen. He doesn't know what our office/my attorney is like." You can make it happen. How? Read on.

B. Protecting and Using Your Time

Getting Real

Certainly, before we can make your plan a reality we need to know what your present reality is, so we can determine what needs to be changed. This will require another chart. This time we'll use seven columns labeled as indicated in Figure 1.11. In the first column of the first row, list the first task for today in your Plan, for example, "check voicemail." In the second column list the amount of time you allocated for this task in your plan, say, six minutes or one-tenth of an hour. Skip the next column for now. In the fourth column write the present time and start the task. Chances are you can make it through this task without interruption. Enter the time you end it in the fifth column and then enter the Real Task Time in the third column. Check out Figure 1.11 to see what I mean.

Now let's try something harder—getting through the mail. Enter "Open and Sort Mail" in the first column of the second row. Enter the start time and get to it! This time chances, are you won't make it through the task without a delay—emails, telephone calls, intercom, people stopping by. Record each delay in the sixth column and how long the delay took from you and your plan in the last column. (See Figure 1.11)

Figure 1.11: Chart Showing Effects of Interruptions
on Task Completion Time

Task	Time	Real Time	Start	Finish	Delay	Delay Time
Check voicemail	.1	.1	8:06	8:11		
Open and sort mail	.3	1.0	8:12	9:12	Email from office manager—reviewed and deleted	.1
					Call from client A	.2
					Email from John asking you to meet him for lunch— calendar checked, reply sent	.1
					Intercom from Jane checking on status of mail. Discussed weekend.	.1
					Intercom from attorney reminding me Johnson will is due on Wednesday	.1
					Look for Johnson file. Realize attorney notes are not in file. Go to attorney's office; retrieve notes, post to file.	.4

OK. It's now 9:24 and you have just finished the task your Plan says should have been done by about 8:30! It took almost an hour to do what should only take about 15 minutes.

Now you are really stressed. Wait a minute. Take a deep breath. Your Plan is a Plan. Actually, it's more than that, it's Your Plan. But the idea is to reduce stress, not add to it. In order to reduce stress, we need to know what is causing it.

Interruptions and Lack of Organization

Interruptions and lack of organization are a major boon for the pharmaceutical industry. They account for a lot of the need for medication to reduce stress and reduce the effects of stress. It took an hour to open and sort the mail because other people and lack of organization used up YOUR time.

You could, and should, continue the Real Time Chart for a typical day. It will help you to know what the sources of interruptions and the areas lacking organization are in your day. Once you know that information you can protect your time, use your time effectively and organize your work in a way that will make your Plan happen. We'll discuss your time in this chapter and your work in the next.

Protecting and Using Your Time

You cannot manage your time if someone else is using it. I'm not suggesting you get huffy with the other staff or your attorney about this, but I am suggesting that you and your attorney should set appropriate boundaries to protect, and efficiently use, your and your attorney's time.

Many days it seems as though everyone wants a part of your day. It seems that way because it is, for practical purposes, true. Voicemail, email and instant messaging are wonderful inventions, but they do make it easier for those who want a part of your day to make a grab for it.

Email is primary offender and not just for you. Large businesses complain that they deal with about 100 million incoming messages on a monthly basis. They take measures to deal with the influx, such as limiting the size of employee mailboxes. You can take measures, too.

Since email is such a large offender, let's focus on it. It'd be nice to simply turn it off, but let's face facts: it is useful and often actually important, so we need a more measured solution. However, the fact that email is important doesn't mean that each email is important. In fact, some email deserves no attention and none of our time. Fortunately, even major software companies recognize that spam is a problem and provide mechanisms for filtering it. Check your email program and set the spam filter at a level that works for you. It is better to set it high and filter out too many emails, than to let bothersome email through. Check your spam folder periodically and authorize emails from those you want to receive. You are likely to hear from them anyway when they call to say you haven't answered their email.

Speak to your attorney and office manager about programs that block spam. They are not very expensive and are almost certainly less costly than paying you to deal with spam on an individual email basis. Also, you aren't the only one in the office dealing with spam. The cost of a software program to deal with it is very likely to be less than the cost of paying everyone to deal with spam emails on an individual basis.

Not all bothersome email deserving little or no attention is spam. Some of it comes from *inside* your office. Do you really need to be included in every inter-office communication just because it's easier to hit Reply All rather than Reply? Do you need to pay *immediate* attention to emails from the office manager reminding you of the date for the office picnic? I could list dozens of examples, but I don't want to take up more of your time. Instead, let's take control of email.

Email Options

Almost all email programs have options which allow you to control email. The first is the Delete key. You are not obligated to read and respond to every email you get from someone in the office. Just as some tasks can be removed from your task list, some email can simply be ignored or at least stored until a time more convenient to you. Take advantage of the Delete key. Certainly there are some emails that cannot be ignored. You know who sends them and you know the information that the subject line will contain. The rest can be either deleted or moved out of your Inbox to be read at a more convenient time.

Email Rules

There are also "Rules." Again, almost every email program has a Rules function even if it's called something else. Since the most popular program is Outlook, I'll focus on it. The goal is to immediately move all email other than that which requires your immediate attention out of the Inbox. Since we don't want it in the Inbox, we need to create a place for it to go. The good news is we can create several such places.

In Outlook, click on "Inbox," so that it is selected, i.e., highlighted. Then click on File in the toolbar. This will bring up a menu that includes New Folder. Click on New Folder. You can name this folder whatever makes sense to you. Are many of your "I don't need to deal with this now" emails from the paralegal down the hall? Name the folder after that paralegal. Or simply name it "24 hours" indicating you will deal with the email within the next day. You can have other folder for other people or other folders indicating the relative importance of the email.

Now we get to the fun part. You can, and should, create Rules that govern your email. In the Tools menu (Outlook 2003) click Rules and Alerts. Now you can create a rule governing how your email will work. All emails from particular persons or with particular subjects can be directed never to enter your Inbox at all! You can read them and respond to them when you want and if you want. You can create a rule directing emails to your Junk Mail folder, but be careful with this one.

You even have choices on email that *is* important. For example, every email I send my paralegals is important. I expect each one to be read and, if appropriate, to engender a response. However, my paralegal can chose how to deal with that expectation. My emails can go directly to the Inbox with an alert announcing their arrival, or they can go to a folder with my name—a clear indication of just how important they are.

Then there are emails in the middle. Now that offices run on email communications, it is often necessary to communicate by email. But you don't have to communicate with the sender every time they chose to communicate with you. If you create a folder and rule for each sender with whom you want to communicate regularly, you can check that folder periodically. Outlook lets you know how many new messages you have from that sender.

If you create folders and rules for emails from people you want or need to communicate with, you need to let them know. For this communication personal contact is better than email. Before you speak to them, figure out what will work for you. If you are going to check their folders when you start the day, at 11:00 a.m., 2:00 p.m., and at the end of the day, let them know what you are doing and why.

It's best not to make this personal. Discuss it with your attorney first. Then let each person know you are establishing these rules for everyone so you can control your day. While they may not like the fact that they will not receive immediate attention, they will at least know *why* they are not receiving immediate attention. Be prepared though, for them to do the same. They may decide to create a folder for you and only check it at times that make sense in their day. That's O.K. The more people doing this in your office, the better it will work.

If you work with this for awhile, you'll discover more ways to control your email. In fact, many of the concepts used to control email can be used to control other interruptions. Let's take a look at phone calls.

Managing Phone Calls

This is tricky. First of all, in most law offices, you, the paralegal, are the primary means of managing the attorney's phone calls. Any procedure for managing your incoming calls will require a frank discussion with the attorney and, perhaps, with the entire office management. Second, many of your calls can't simply be ignored the way we're going to ignore many emails. As we discussed before, clients are the mainstay of a law practice. Ignoring them is not good.

Ignoring phone calls is one thing. Managing them is another. There are times when taking phones calls is tremendously disruptive to doing other important work and times when it has little disruptive effect at all. There are also many times that fit in between these two extremes. You, and to a degree, your attorney, are best suited to determine which times are which.

Phone Rules

In most law offices it is taken as a general rule, you do not take phone calls from one client while you are in a meeting with another. You can't take a call from one client while you are on the phone with another. Certainly you can't take phone calls from a client while in a courtroom assisting the attorney.

As a general rule, in each of these situations, what you are doing takes priority over a client's phone call. In each of these situations, both the client and the law practice survive until you are available. In each of these situations, the work you are doing requires your attention and focus in order to be done correctly and timely. There are other such situations, requiring similar general rules.

Drafting Mrs. Johnson's Will, the Smith's deed and the Hunington case Interrogatories all require *concentrated and continuous* attention and focus in order to be done on-time and without error. Interruptions take not only the actual time of the interruption, but the time needed to regain focus. An hour project interrupted five times by three-minute phone calls becomes a two-hour project. The five phone calls only took an extra fifteen minutes, but you also had to make notes for the file for later follow up, perhaps do some immediate follow up, record the time for billing, remember what you were doing before the interruption, review what you had done just before the interruption and so on.

All the while, the deadline for the Will, the Deed or the Interrogatories is approaching. The time you had set aside to do the task is gone and you have to move on to the next appointment. The interruptions caused by the phone calls themselves increase the chances of a mistake. When you get to return to this task, the stress of the approaching deadline increases the opportunity for mistakes even more. More of your attorney's time and your time will be used to correct the mistakes (with luck) before they are noticed by the client, the court or other attorneys.

While these tasks may not seem quite the same as being in a meeting with an actual client, they are similar. Taking a call from one client in such situations is a disservice to the client to whom you are currently attending. Drafting the Will may not have the same priority and sense of immediacy as assisting your attorney in a courtroom, but, as a general rule, it has more priority and should cause more sense of immediacy than taking a call from a client just because the client chose that time to call. So make it a general rule.

There are a couple of ways to accomplish this. One is to set a designated time or designated times each day or each week for doing projects which require continuous, concentrated attention and focus, say Tuesday afternoons from 2 to 4 and Friday mornings from 9 to 11. Another is to work these times into your daily plan each day. Either way, schedule that time just as you would an appointment with the client and let others in the office know that during that time phone calls are to be treated in the same fashion as they would if you were in a client meeting.

Calling Back

When you don't call the client back, the client calls you back. Some clients call back sooner and more often than others. Some are impatient. Some are down right testy and rude. Have some pity on the person at the front desk and make things easier for you at the same time. Establish rules and policies for calling back. More important, establish mechanisms for calling back *and let the client know what those mechanisms are.*

Instruct the receptionist, or if your calls go directly to your voicemail, leave an informative outgoing message, on how calls will be returned. For example, the receptionist might say, "Ms. Forest will be returning clients calls between 2 and 4 this afternoon, can I schedule a telephone appointment for you then?" We will talk more about when to inform your client of this type of device when we discuss managing your clients. For now, make sure any general rules you make about managing your phone calls include both a provision for protecting your time and time for returning the calls.

Shut Your Door

Once you've dealt with emails, voicemails and phone calls, you'll be able to get down to concentrating on work. Until the paralegal next door comes by to tell you about her weekend. Or the secretary from down the hall stops in to ask if you want to contribute to the baby gift for Mary's baby shower next Friday. Or the guy from down in finance stops by to see if you want to take a spot in the office Final Four pool.

There may even be people coming by to discuss work. The new paralegal wants your opinion on how to deal with a difficult client. The secretary wants to know if you have any of those special covers for legal briefs going to the appeals court. The guy down in payroll wants to discuss your 401(k) options.

Either way, you won't get your work done on time. Shut your door. Not all day. Just long enough to finish the project you need to finish. Put the necessary time on your calendar and the office calendar so others can see you have to focus on a client's work. Let others know what you are doing and why. Discuss it with your attorney and/or the office manager in advance.

Lighten Up

Other than some organizing specifically related to managing your calendar or docket, your files, your clients or your attorney, you are now ready to come in at 8:00 a.m. and work efficiency and effectively straight through to 5:00 p.m. You can start the day by implementing your "Interruption Control" techniques while you set out your plan for the day and revise your plan for the next seven days. You can schedule every task down to the minute and schedule every minutes from clocking in at 8 and clocking out at 5. Your desk will be pristine throughout the day, holding only the file you are working on and the exact tools you need to complete the scheduled task on that file.

DON'T DO IT. For your sake, for your attorney's sake and for the sake of your family, lighten up.

Do talk to your coworkers about weekends, baby showers, the Super Bowl and *Survivor*. Get out of your office and walk around the block. Add a few pictures of your family to your workplace. Pin up that picture of a cat your daughter drew in kindergarten last week. I even like to use some of that closed door time to sneak in a bit of a "power nap."

Managing your time does not mean turning yourself into a computerized robot. It means, within the parameters of your office's policies, utilizing techniques which allow you to be human while efficiently and effectively completing your work. In fact, you may even find that being able to control your time while accomplishing your work makes you feel good.

C. Tracking and Billing Your Time

By now you probably have learned how important keeping time records are to a law firm. Most law firms finance their operations by billing clients for time, generally referred to as "billable hours," spent on the client's matter. Sometimes, particular matters are handled with other fee arrangements. The two most common are contingency fees and flat-rate fees.

Contingency fees are most common in personal injury cases. In these cases, fees are a percentage, often 33.3% of the amount collected for the client. If, for any reason, no money is collected for the client, then there is no fee. For example, if two cars collide at an intersection and both drivers claim to have a green light, only one driver will be believed by the jury and only that driver will be awarded compensation for her injuries. Only that driver's attorney will collect a fee. Some firms handle only personal injury cases and operate totally based on contingency fees.

Some work is done on the flat-rate fee basis. This is common in law practices based on real estate where there may be a set fee for providing a deed, another fee for certifying title, another set fee for attending a closing, and so on.

Tracking Time for Client Work

Even when fee arrangements are not directly tied to time expended on a client matter, it is important to keep track of time expended for each client. There are several reasons for this.

For example, in most jurisdictions there are formal rules governing contingency fee agreements. Those rules state that attorneys can only charge reasonable fees. Many jurisdictions require attorneys to submit fee disputes to a Fee Arbitration panel if the client requests such submission. Whether the reasonableness of the fees is determined by a judge, a jury or a fee arbitration panel, the amount of time expended on the case is a major component of the determination.

Another reason is more practical. Assume a firm must receive $40 dollars per hour for a paralegal's time in order to take in the money necessary to pay the paralegal's salary, benefits, worker's compensation insurance, unemployment compensation contribution, workspace overhead and so on, but bills on a flat-rate basis for deeds. If they are billing $75.00 for each deed, but each deed is taking two hours, the firm has a problem.

The firm needs to take some action. It can raise the price of a deed to $80.00. It can find ways to reduce the time it takes for the paralegal to do a deed, perhaps purchasing new software. It can stop doing deeds as a part of its law practice, leaving that type of work to firms that do a higher volume of real estate work. It can decide to continue the deed practice as it is a "loss leader" to draw in clients, and make up the difference in another area.

In any case, it must *do something* or it will be unable to meet its expenses. That means it will be unable to pay *you*. We do not want that to happen. The only way the firm will know it has a problem with deeds is for the attorneys and paralegals to track their time.

Tracking Time for Non-Client Work

There are third and fourth reasons for you to track your time that are more practical to you. They involve non-billable time, that is, time not necessarily spent on client work.

Several sections ago, I suggested that some of your tasks may be better handled by someone with less skill than you. This may require hiring another full or part-time staff member. You may recall me warning you that convincing your attorney or office manager that this was the right thing to do would require some initiative on your part. Tracking your time may very well give you the ammunition your need.

Really, did you get your paralegal degree to spend time filing? That alone is enough reason for you to track the time. But we're not done yet.

We started this chapter with you doing a Job Description Chart that including estimates of the amount of time you spent doing particular tasks. We moved on to making plans and schedules to structure and manage time in a way that makes sense given the work you do. Up to now it's been a matter of guess work.

The guess work is quite educated because you have a good grasp of your job and what it entails. After all, you do the job day in and day out. However, really effective time management requires that you *know* how much time it takes to do a task. You can't plan an allotted amount of time for filing each week if you don't know how much time you actually spend filing each week.

Finally, it's your time. You can gain a great deal of satisfaction from knowing how you are using it and knowing you are managing it well.

D. Ethical Considerations

I know people have been harping at you about ethical considerations since *Introduction to Paralegal Studies*. And it is difficult to see how there can be ethical considerations to simply managing your time. As I have been saying all along it is *your* time.

Right. I agree, but ethics is a part of life so we will take a few minutes at the end of each chapter to consider some of the many ways ethical considerations apply to the topic of that chapter.

First, it is your time and you get to choose how you use it to do your job. Your job is to assist your attorney and your attorney must place the client's interest first. While you have the power to set your schedule, make plans and manage time to most effectively perform your work, keep in mind that your work is to advance your clients' interests. That sounds simple enough and usually is, so we'll move on.

Second, it is your time, but the law firm is paying for it. I think the best paralegal from the stand point of cost/benefit considerations is one who is happy and satisfied with his work. Being happy and satisfied in your work requires many things, most of which are beyond the scope of this book. Some job satisfaction factors emanating from time management have already been mentioned, for example in the "Lighten Up" section. Others will be discussed later.

If your attorney and office manager read this book, they'll probably agree with me. We'll discuss how to deal with this issue a bit more in the chapter on managing your attorney. In the meantime, you need to manage your time within the parameters set by your employer. When all is said and done, you have an ethical obligation to your employer to give them an honest day's work for an honest day's pay. It is not only an ethical duty; it is part of being a professional.

The last and most explicit ethical consideration arises from tracking and billing time. In most instances, the client is paying for your and your attorney's time. There are many opportunities in most law practices for "double billing." Double billing is not an ethical practice in most jurisdictions and is specifically prohibited by the ABA (American Bar Association) Model Rules. The Model Rules are not legally binding, but they are good guidelines for judging behavior ethically. Chances are your jurisdiction has a similar rule which is binding on your attorney.

Picture yourself waiting at the courthouse for the judge and attorneys to complete an in-chambers conference on jury instructions. What better time to start drafting a motion to dismiss on your next case? There may be no better time, but be aware that ethically you cannot bill that time to both the client on trial and the client for whom you are drafting the complaint.

Perhaps the motion to dismiss on your next case is based upon the same case law as the motion to dismiss on the case in trial. That makes it easy. You can just dig out the research you did on the case in trial and use it to do the motion on the new case. But be careful how you bill for the work. Feel free to use that legal research so you can be efficient and fast in completing this task. But if you already billed that legal research to the first client you can't ethically bill it again to the new client. That is also double billing.

Ultimately it is your attorney's and your law office's responsibility to decide how to bill. It is your responsibility to keep honest time records. In general, don't bill more than one client for the same time and don't bill the more than one client for the same work. You'll be fine.

Conclusion

That's it for this chapter. The next chapters will often apply the same concepts to other aspects of your career as a paralegal. But before moving on, sit back and take a deep breath. Better yet, get up and move around. Walk around the block. Have a snack.

You've got time.

Chapter Two

Managing Your Work—It's a Mess, but It's MY Mess!

A. Organizing Your Work and Your Workplace

In almost every office of moderate or larger size and in many smaller offices, there is an office that has it door closed all the time because it would be an embarrassment for clients to see it. Let's call the owner of this office "Joe." There are files, documents, unopened mail, ancient unread copies of the ABA Journal, Wall Street Journal, the state bar journal and advertisements for legal and non-legal journals of every type and description on every horizontal surface. Unopened boxes of USCA pocket-part updates are stuck in the corners and under chairs. There are not even a few inches of open space on the desk. When visitors enter the office, Joe, somewhat embarrassed, gestures futilely towards a chair. The gesture is futile because there is far too much clutter on the chair for anyone to attempt sitting there.

It is not the workplace of an empowered, effective paralegal. This workplace controls the worker even to the extent of requiring him to move sideways to avoid knocking papers onto the floor. The empowered, effective paralegal controls the workplace, rather than let it control her.

Of course, this isn't *your* workplace, but most of us have some parts of it in our workplaces. So in this chapter we will start you on the path to organizing your work and workplace by working together to figuratively take control of this one. We will start the same way we started with task and emails. We will identify, sort, prioritize and delete.

First, though, we need to (1) set a time to accomplish our task and (2) let the front desk know what to do about calls while we're doing this.

Some of Joe's stuff may be important. Some may still need attention right away. Some will need attention in the next few days. Some will need attention down the road a bit. Some has already been handled and will need to be filed in the appropriate client file. Some, probably much, can simply be dragged to the recycling bin. That means we need four "clear spots" and a recycling bin. As we sort through Joe's things, we will place them in one of the four spots or toss them in recycling.

Deleting

Our basic operating principle will be that each item belongs in recycling unless there's a good reason to put it somewhere else. For example, Joe, like most people in business, subscribes to relevant journals, such as the local paralegal association newsletter and the national paralegal journals. Someday, he assures himself, he'll read them. Honestly though, if he has not read last month's issue by the time this month's arrived, he's not going to read it no matter how long it sits on the desk. Somewhat in recognition of this principle, he has moved older issues to a chair, even older issues to the top of the filing cabinet and the oldest to the floor in the corner.

We'll move all but this month's issue to the recycling bin. We'll do the same with newspapers and the like. Make a note to yourself to do the same when you return to your office. Tomorrow, when you've gained control of your time and work, you'll have time to read newspapers and journals as they arrive.

Sorting and Prioritizing

Suddenly the task is far less intimidating. We have reduced clutter by about half. We have even created some clear spots to put things belonging to other categories. And we still have time left to begin sorting and prioritizing the rest. You can empty the recycling bin, but bring it back. I bet we will still have use for it. Hidden among the piles of official looking documents are all those special offers on credit cards and advertisements for even more journals and last year's seminars.

When we get done deleting, we will also be done sorting and prioritizing because the deletion process is part of the overall organizing process. As we noted before, some of the remaining papers may still need attention right away. We will be left will four fairly small piles of papers and files. Some will need attention in the next few days. Some will need attention down the road a bit. Some has already been handled and will need to be filed in the appropriate client file or in the proper file cabinet.

In fact, the documents in these piles are likely to be small enough in number and bulk to put into file folders. Try manila expandable folders if the standard manila ones are not quite large enough. We will use the brownish colored expandable ones if necessary. Label one "Today," one "To Be Determined Today," one "This Week," and one "To Be Filed." The various piles of rubble have now been reduced to four folders placed neatly on the desk! That's too many folders to have on a desk.

Let's face it, none of us can really do more than one thing at a time if, unlike breathing which is instinctive or walking which has been so often performed it is imprinted, it actually requires attention. Multitasking makes it look like several things are being done at once, but actually the tasks are being broken down into components, then the components are being done individually in rapid succession. At any one point, one or more tasks are not getting the attention it or they should get, or at least would get if it were the only task being performed. Overall, this is a less efficient method of working than simply focusing on one thing and getting it done.

Since we can only work on one item, there should only be one item on our desk. In most instances the item will be a client file. In some instances we can "cheat" a bit and call "the mail" one item. In Joe's case, the "Today" folder is one item; the "To Be Determined Today" folder is another, and so on. Leave the figurative "Today" folder on his desk with an imaginary note explaining what we have done and where all his stuff is.

The other folders can be put away until he is ready to work on them. If Joe is smart, before putting them away he will select a time to deal with them and enter that time on his calendar. Stuff in the "To Be Filed" folder is more likely to move out of that folder and into the files if a time, say tomorrow at 10 a.m., is set for getting it done.

In the meantime it should be removed from the desk and put in *its* place. Since Joe won't be getting to the "To Be Determined Today" file right away (he has to deal with the "Today" file first), it too should be put in its place until he is ready to deal with it. We will discuss where that place is in *your* workplace soon.

Incoming Mail

Incoming mail, whatever its source, is essentially "To Be Determined Today" fodder. I use the term "incoming mail" loosely here as it applies to everything that comes into your workplace from a source other than you—FedEx, your attorney, the secretary—not just mail arriving through the United States Postal Service.

The USPS mail differs from the rest in that it usually arrives at a regular time and only once or twice a day, making it easier to schedule a time to handle it. However, other deliveries should, in general, be treated the same in terms of the way it is handled. Other deliveries differ from USPS mail only in the randomness of their arrival. In this sense, such deliveries are more like email or phone calls. They are random interruptions. Establish procedures for dealing with them as you have with those other interruptions. For the most part, the fact that other people chose to deliver these things to you now does not impose upon you an obligation to deal with them *now* other than by subjecting it to whatever procedure you have established for that priority.

When you do deal with the mail, *deal with it.* Don't just open it and stick it in a pile. Use the same approach we used to clear Joe's work place. Start by deleting. Make each item justify its imposition on your time. If it does not, toss it.

Now that you are managing your time better, you will have time to read the newspaper, newsletters and some of those journals. But really, will you ever read them all? Consider canceling some subscriptions or having them go to the office library. Continue the ones you either really need to read or really want to read. Most important, if you haven't read the last issue when this issue arrives either schedule time to read the last issue or get rid of it.

Use the same quick judgment with any other item that is potential trash. Advertisements, brochures, solicitations, reminders and the like all qualify. Is there an actual reason to hold on to it? Remember, anything you hold onto you have to do something with. We are not going to let it just sit in a pile on your desk or anywhere else.

Now we are down to the Real Mail: letters and other documents that actually relate to your work. If it relates to your work, then it most likely relates to a client file. That means it either has to go into a client file or it requires some action on the part of your office. If it goes into a client file, put it in the "To Be Filed" folder. If you have not been able to convince your attorney and/or office manager to hire that part-time student to do the filing, remember to schedule time to do the filing.

If it requires action on the part of your office, you have a few options. First, note that I said it requires action *on the part of your office*—not necessarily you. Your first option is to limit your contact with the item to determining who in your office should do the action and getting the item to that person— your attorney, another paralegal, a secretary, file clerk, the office manager, etc. If you regularly receive a lot of this kind of mail, it may make sense to have folders available to hold the items until you are done sorting the mail. It might be one folder labeled "Deliver to Others," or a separate folder for each recipient. The important thing is that it not become clutter in your workplace.

If it will take some time to do whatever needs to be done, and *you* have to do it, you still have at least a couple of options. One is to place it in the "Today" folder. If it is not going to be done today, then maybe it really should have gone in the "To Be Filed" folder. You need to remember to take action with regard to the item, but you don't need the item as a reminder. Soon such reminders just become clutter. Enter it on one of your three "To Do Lists." I know you probably don't have three "To Do Lists" yet, but you will by the end of this chapter.

Just Do It

Before stating the final option, let's take a look at the common factor in all the previous options. Whether you are deleting an item or placing it in one of the folders, you are disposing of the item fairly quickly. There will be some items, possibility the majority of the mail, where the action required by you is not much more time consuming than, say, placing the item in the "To Be Delivered" folder and doing the delivery. In these cases, just do it.

At least one time management expert refers to this option as the "Three Minute Rule." Time is managed well by organization, but good time management practices should also include simplification and accomplishment. Indeed, the ultimate goal of time management is to enable accomplishment of your work in a timely way. If you can complete a task fairly quickly now, now is the time to accomplish that task. Keep in mind that you will be including such action as a component of the "Open Mail" task when scheduling time to open the mail.

If filing in your office is a complex task requiring going to a file room, hole-punching the document and adding it to the index, then create and use a "To Be Filed" folder. If filing means pulling out a file drawer two steps from your desk and adding the item to the front of the file folder, *just do it.* (As we discuss in Chapter Four, I do not recommend the latter as it results in cluttered, unmanageable files. Even if the file is in that nearby file drawer, take the time to properly enter and record the document in the file.)

If the title company is asking you to check with your attorney, your client, the seller and the seller's attorney to arrange a date and time for closing, put the letter in the "Today" folder or put it away and add the task to a "To Do" list. If the title company is notifying you that the closing has been scheduled and all you have to do is add it to your calendar and your attorney's calendar, *just do it,* (assuming that you have a procedure in place for notifying the client based on such a calendar entry).

If a letter requests information that will require retrieving a file, doing research and writing a letter, then put the letter in the "Today" folder or put it away and add the task to a "To Do" list. If you can check boxes on a form, copy the form near your office and place the form in a self-addressed envelope provided by the sender of the letter, *just do it.*

B. If I Had a Hammer...

You don't need a hammer to do your job, or at least most paralegals do not. But there are many tools or implements you do need—computer, stapler, paper clips, hole-punch, file folders and so on. Now that you are done opening the mail, your desk, like Joe's, is clear except for the one file on which you are about to work. Well, it is probably not that *clear*. There's only one file, but there is a lot of other stuff on it. Stuff is OK. We just want to organize and manage it.

We'll start with another priority list. This one only needs two columns. In the first list the tools you need to do you job. In the second indicate how often you need that tool. You can be fairly loose about classification on this list. The second column can range from "All the time," through "Pretty often," "Often," "Not Very Often," "Only when I'm forced to" to "Almost never."

There is a branch of science called "ergonomics." Basically, ergonomists study human capabilities in relationship to work demands. The term "ergonomics" is derived from two Greek words: "ergon," meaning work and "nomoi," meaning natural laws. Ergonomists help design your workplace so you maintain good posture, avoid carpal tunnel syndrome and the like. In many places the insurance company providing your employer with Worker's Compensation insurance will have expert ergonomists come to your workplace and provide a free analysis. I highly recommend you take advantage of this service if it is available.

I don't do ergonomics. I really do not know that much about ergonomics. Right now we just want you to have a workplace that is well organized so you can get your work done efficiently and effectively; to allow you to control your workplace rather than have it control you.

So sit in your chair. Reach forward. Reach to your sides. Swivel in your chair and reach behind you. All the tools you marked "All the time" should be within your reach. Most likely the only tools you really use somewhat all the time are the computer and the telephone. These should not only be in your reach but in front of you with space allotted for the file on which you are working. Those next in line can be off to one side or the other with the ones used more frequently on your dominate side. Lesser used tools can be behind you.

Anything used less than once or twice a week should be put away. When you get ready to do the once or twice a week task requiring that tool, get it out. Then put it away when you are done. My grandmother would have made this all a lot simpler. She would have told you "A place for everything and everything in its place." I want to encourage you to find a place that makes sense in terms of the use you make of the tool and the frequency with which you use it.

C. To Do Lists

Other than our brief discussion of deleting some items from your task list, we have focused on organizing your time, your work and your workplace so you have control, i.e., so you have the power to get your work correctly done in an efficient, timely and effective way. Few, if any, of your tasks have disappeared.

While we prioritized your tasks in a general sense by category or type, we still need a way to see that the individual tasks related to your actual client files get done. You cannot do your daily schedule based on averages or the normal times it takes to get things done. Scheduling an hour to draft deeds this week only makes sense if you actually have deeds to draft this week.

Looking at this from the other direction, filing away mail that requires some action only makes sense if there is a way to record and remind yourself of what action needs to be done. Some of these actions will be very important, but also may be a long way off. For example, the discovery deadline in a case may be six months away, or a closing on a real estate sale may be ninety days down the road. These dates need to go on a calendar with a "tickler" so the component parts of those tasks get started in time to complete by the deadline. We will discuss this more in Chapter Three.

There are other tasks that are more immediate. Things you need to get done today; those that need to get done tomorrow; and those that need to be done soon. "Soon" can mean this week, ten days or this month, depending on your particular workload. You need a way to record and remind yourself of these tasks. "To Do" lists make serve this function.

At the beginning of the day when you open the mail, check email, check voicemail, take phone calls, speak with your attorney and review the calendar, you will note actions that you must accomplish *today*. Make a list of those tasks. Some, such as "Meet with Mrs. Johnson at 10:00" are "pre-scheduled." Other such as "Get additional information from doctor's office on Mr. Jones' injury" can be worked into the schedule. Take a few minutes to review all these items and your other To Do Lists and make a daily schedule that makes sense.

If you attempt to schedule all of today's To Do List items today and cannot, then take a few more minutes to make a plan. Can some of the items be put off until tomorrow if you make arrangements with the client, your attorney, an opposing attorney or the title company? Can you enlist assistance from someone else in the office? If there is truly a problem dealing with today's To Do List today, deal with the problem right off. Most important, let your attorney know there is a problem.

Do not let items not placed on today's To Do List simply float around. They belong on tomorrow's To Do List, the Soon To Do List or the tickler calendar.

You can, and should, make the decision as to when they are best handled, but you want to make the decision rather than let events make the decision for you.

There are many software programs designed to assist with managing Task To Do Lists. Even standard computer packages such as Outlook have fairly sophisticated Task tracking programs. Other programs are specifically designed for law offices and combine these functions with others useful to the practice of law. There are also many non-computer connected products such as Day-Timers available at the local office supply store useful in keeping track of both your calendar and tasks.

I highly recommend using these products to assist you in managing your tasks. However, even if none of these products are available to you, you can and must take control of your work. This requires organizing your time, your workplace and your tasks. Simple desk calendars and "To Do" lists can serve this purpose, if you make them work by creating and using them.

Conclusion

Survey your new domain. It's well organized, neat and clean. In fact, it may be a bit too sterile. You've taken control, the work and the workspace is yours, but it isn't quite "You." Add in a few of the photos, plants or knick-knacks that make you feel at home while at work, keeping in mind that you are a professional and you are at work, not at home or in your college dorm. The key word here is "few." You do not want to replace paper clutter with tchotchkes.

Now you are ready to get to work. But first, add a time to your calendar near the end of each week to re-establish your office organization. Try as you might to keep it organized as you go along, the forces of chaos will intrude. Fifteen minutes at the end of the week will allow you to re-assess and re-impose your organization. Then take a few more minutes to reward yourself. Get a cup of coffee, get out this month's issue of *Litigation Paralegal* and read a bit before it's time to put it into recycling.

You've got the time and the place.

CHAPTER THREE

MANAGING YOUR DOCKET/ CALENDAR—TWICE IS NICE!

Deadlines. Dreaded deadlines. Deadly deadlines. Damn deadlines. We could spend the day repeating the many alliterative references for deadlines. If not managed correctly, they can lead to scenes like this:

Amanda and Hank are stressing out. Todd Johnson, the attorney for whom they work, starts trial tomorrow the matter of <u>Weir v Hasselback</u> and there's a lot to be done. The Pre-trial Management Order requires that all Motions in Limine, Requests for Jury Instructions and Special Verdict Forms be filed on the first morning of trial. Some witnesses need to be subpoenaed. Exhibits need to be prepared and marked for identification.

Meanwhile, in another matter, a Scheduling Order deadline for designation of expert witnesses is looming for Monday. Amanda, Hank and Todd will all still be tied up by the Hasselback trial at least until Tuesday. To top it off, Answers to Interrogatories are due in the matter of <u>Jones v Lopez</u> next Thursday. The Hasselback trial should be over by then, but Lopez hasn't corrected and returned the first draft as yet.

Fortunately, Amanda and Hank know how to do all the work they have to do. That knowledge came with their paralegal degree and from additional on-the-job training. Unfortunately, they just don't see how they can do it all by the deadlines. They have come to believe that this sort of last minute stress is inevitable and have learned to deal with such stress in a professional way.

Since there appears to be no better way to handle situations like this, they already have a fairly good idea how it's all going to get done. They are staying late again tonight. They already called home to unhappy partners and children and gave fair warning.

There is a better way. Let's change the perspective on deadlines so we can deal with them rather than dread them.

A. Understanding Deadlines

Deadlines seem to run directly opposite to our efforts to manage our work. Most of them are imposed by someone else—a court, a client, a bank, a boss. We have little or no control over them. You *can* control how you manage them and plan for meeting them.

Some deadlines are not really recognized as deadlines. Deadlines are just dates by which something must be done; marks on a calendar. When the mark records something we want to do, say a vacation, we tend not to view it as a deadline.

Let's pretend you have a brother or sister living hundreds of miles from you. She or he is getting married in a month and you are to be in the wedding party. You have a lot to do in order to attend the wedding and it must all be done before the date of the wedding. That date is a deadline—meet it and you attend the wedding; miss it and the wedding photos will have a blank spot where you should be.

Chances are you don't view the wedding as a "deadline," but you do treat it as one. You make at least a mental list of what needs to be done and make a plan to get them done. Buy a gift. Rent a tux/buy a dress. Make a plane reservation. Arrange for a place to stay. Maybe you enlist the help of your siblings. Then you begin making at least mental notes on how to do each of the necessary tasks.

What gift will you get? Where will you get the gift? You find out more information. What hotels are available near the wedding? Where are the bride and groom registered for gifts? What are the requirements for that dress or tux? This additional information allows you to refine your overall plan.

Finally, you develop a plan for accomplishing each task. If your plane leaves at 10:00 a.m., what time do you need to get to the airport? What time do you have to leave your home for the airport? Allow time and money for parking or taking a cab. Ship the gift or take it with you?

You work all this into your calendar between other things you need to do. Or perhaps, you make other arrangements for the other things on your calendar.

As you sit at the reception toasting the bride and groom, your focus in on them, rather than the competency with which you met the deadline they set for you!

B. Six Easy and Essential Steps for Meeting Deadlines

1. *Make a list of the component parts necessary to meet your goal.* Going to the wedding required a gift, a dress or tux, transportation and a place to

stay. Holding a closing requires a deed, probably a mortgage or deed of trust, a title search, title insurance and so on, just as starting a trial may require motions, witness subpoenas and jury instructions. This step is similar to the first step in managing your time in Chapter One and your workload in Chapter Two. There will be other similarities as we proceed.

2. *Record essential time requirements on your calendar.* Record not just the dates on which you need to be at the wedding, start the trial, hold the closing or execute the will, but the dates on which each essential component must be accomplished. You'll want the hotel reservations for the wedding well before getting on the plane. You'll need a title opinion before getting title insurance. You need a description of the property before getting title opinion.

3. *Make a plan for accomplishing each component on your list.* Just as you needed a plan for getting to the airport, you need a plan for getting the subpoenas served on time or the title opinion in. This may initially require finding additional information. Who will serve the subpoenas or exam the title records? How much lead time do they need? If necessary, break these tasks down into smaller components with their own plan.

4. *Record the date on which you must START each part of your plan in order to complete it on time.* Build in time for the unexpected whether it's the cab getting stuck in traffic on the way to the airport, a witness being out of town, or the title examiner needing more lead time than originally indicated.

5. *Establish reminders for each for each start and end date.* It's not enough to mark the calendar. We all need "ticklers" to remind us as we go along. In fact, we sometimes become complacent about deadlines because they are on the calendar. More on this when we discuss calendar systems.

6. *Review your entire calendar and integrate the new plan into the overall management of your work.* Look at events before, during and after the deadline. If the new event will chew up time you had planned to use completing a task for meeting another deadline, you may need to change one or both plans. When Amanda, Hank and Todd received the notice for trial on the Hasselback case, a review of the calendar would have let them know they needed to change the plan (assuming they had a plan) for getting the Lopez interrogatories completed on time.

In Chapter One we considered the example of Mrs. Johnson's Will. Once the information needed to complete a Will is available, there are still several steps left in the process. The paralegal often prepares of draft of the Will, reviews the draft with the attorney, finalizes the Will, arranges and confirms witnesses and attends the execution of the Will. Notice how the Weekly Plan provided for each of these steps and integrated them into the week's other events. (See Figure 3.1)

Figure 3.1

WEEK OF JANUARY 5, 2009

	Monday	Tuesday	Wednesday	Thursday	Friday
8:00	Make Daily & Weekly Plan	Make Daily Plan & Adjust Weekly Plan	Make Daily Plan & Adjust Weekly Plan	Make Daily Plan & Adjust Weekly Plan	Make Daily Plan, Begin Next Week's Plan
8:30	Mail & Voice Mail Review	Mail & Voice Mail Review	Mail & Voice Mail Review	Mail & Voice Mail Review	Mail & Voice Mail Review
9:00	Meet with Attorney— Coordinate Plans and	*Finalize Jones Will—Arrange for witnesses*		Draft Smith Discovery	
9:30	Responsibilities for week	–		Draft Smith Discovery	
10:00				Draft Smith Discovery	
10:30	Previously Scheduled				
11:00	Client Meeting		*Confirm Witnesses for Jones Will Execution*		
11:30	Lunch	Lunch		Previously Scheduled	Lunch
12:00	*Draft*		Lunch	Client Meeting	
12:30	*Johnson*		With John		
1:00	*Will for attorney to review at 1:30*			Lunch	
1:30	*Meet with Attorney— Review Jones Will*	Previously Scheduled	*Johnson Will Execution*		
2:00		Client			
2:30		Meeting			
3:00	Return Calls	Return Calls	Return Calls	Return Calls	Return Calls
3:30	To Clients & Adjuster	To Clients & Adjuster	To Clients & Adjuster	To Clients & Adjuster	To Clients & Adjuster
4:00		Meet with Attorney— Prep for Wed. Hearings		Meet with Attorney— Review Smith Discovery Draft	
4:30					
5:00	Daily Filing	Daily Filing	Daily Filing	Daily Filing	Daily Filing

The bottom line here is to control and manage how you meet deadlines, not let them control you. Let's move on to some of the mechanisms to assist in that control and management we touched up in the Six Steps.

C. Dual Calendar Systems—Dual Attorney/Paralegal Responsibilities

You can and must manage your calendar. You also have some responsibility for managing your attorney's calendar because you and your attorney are a team. The good news is that you and your attorney are a team, so the attorney also has responsibility for managing the attorney's calendar and some responsibility for managing yours.

Deadlines aren't disastrous or dreadful. *Missed* deadlines are both. Cases, clients and law office reputations are lost due to late filing of documents. Even worse, jobs are lost. Take heart, there are systems designed to minimize this danger. When such systems are chosen and modified by you, your attorney and your office to suit your office's practice, they can practically eliminate the danger. When your chosen system is combined with effective time, work, client and attorney management techniques and double-checking, missing a deadline should be a very rare occurrence indeed.

Calendar Control Systems

The calendar control systems range from very rudimentary to very sophisticated. If your system does not seem to actually be controlling the calendar, find another one that does work for your office.

The basic system is often referred to as the "dual-calendar" system. (There are some systems which are more basic that this, but they do not normally meet the minimum requirements for real calendar control.) In this system, your attorney has a calendar. The attorney should be responsible for making all entries into that system unless you are given responsibility for making specific entries. As we will discuss later, there are some issues on which there should be a clear understanding between you and your attorney. This is one of them.

The "dual" in "dual-calendar" usually refers to a second "office calendar." You may be responsible for entries on this calendar. It may also have entries for other personnel in your office. Especially in an office with two to five attorneys, it is important to know how the demands being made on the entire office's resources.

There is another connotation for the term "dual." You and your attorney should have dual responsibility for ensuring that the calendars are updated *daily*, and that they match one another. You should also have dual responsibility for looking ahead and anticipating problems with meeting deadlines.

I recommend that there be a third calendar—yours. The entries on your calendar may also appear on the office calendar. In fact it is important that both you and your attorney have responsibility for monitoring your calendar. An entry on the office calendar or the attorney's calendar will mean different things to the attorney than it does to you. To the attorney a trial start date may mean preparing an opening statement and preparing witnesses. To you it may mean preparing and having subpoenas served.

So you need your own means of tracking your tasks and managing your workload. Having your attorney become part of your calendaring process will also clue the attorney into just *how much you have to do and when.* This will minimize unrealistic expectations on the part of the attorney and encourage the attorney to engage in the planning necessary to complete tasks on time.

The attorney may have a plan for getting the opening statement and witness preparation done and feel everything is under control. You will also have a plan for getting the subpoenas prepared and served and feel everything is under control. Because you and the attorney are a team, these plans must be coordinated.

Of course, it is also helpful at annual review time for the attorney to have spent the last year fully aware of just how much you do and just how good you are at getting it done on time.

Tickler Systems

Actually not many people call them tickler systems. Some call them "ticklers," others "dairies," others "time index," "perpetual calendars" and so on. Regardless of what your office calls it, have one and use it. Essentially, it is a system that works with and *in addition to* the calendar to "tickle" your memory about upcoming dates. The calendar and tickler are both necessary.

Again, some tickler systems are basic and some are quite sophisticated. One of the most basic uses the old-fashioned index card and index card box set up with dividers for each month and sub-dividers for each day in each month. In some practices, especially those with cases subject to statutes of limitations (deadlines for filing court actions—miss the deadline and you lose the right to sue regardless of the merit or value of your lawsuit) that stretch as far ahead as six years, the index should reach as far ahead as the last deadline.

Each card in the index should contain the name of the client, the name of the matter, the deadline and what needs to be done to meet the deadline. For each task having a deadline there *must* be a card for the start date and the end date.

Some cards will no more than warnings such as "one year warning on statute of limitations," "ninety day warning on expiration of corporate status" or "two year warning on expiration of copyright." These warnings should be keyed to the time likely to be necessary to complete investigations and negotiations and file a lawsuit; obtain the necessary information and file the reports necessary to prevent expiration of corporate status; or complete the copyright renewal process.

Office Policy

The office should have one deadline control system, even if the lawyers practice different fields of law, and it should be used by everyone in the firm. The essence of calendar control systems is cross-checking. Each member of the firm can monitor the calendar for errors, over-commitment of resources and problems arising from unexpected absences of attorneys or staff.

If the office system is not well suited to what your and your attorney do, talk to your attorney and the office manager about adopting a new system. If that doesn't work, maintain your own system separately *and in addition to* the office system. *Do not ignore or neglect the office system.*

D. Software Solutions

By now you know there is a software technology solution to any problem except the problem of paying for the software technology. When it comes to calendar control, there are many possible software solutions. The trick is finding the right solution.

While we're looking for that software solution, let's not give up totally on paper. Sure there are problems with paper calendar systems. For any decent calendar control system you need several paper compilations. There's a calendar for your attorney, one for the office and one for you, plus the tickler even in a one attorney/one paralegal office. Keeping them updated and correlated is a significant project requiring a substantial expenditure of time. When you are done with them, you have to store them, using more time and often valuable space. However, there may be value in having at least one paper calendar, especially one posted where all relevant personnel can see it without booting up the computer.

First, let's take a look at some software options. Software calendars are everywhere. They come with free email services such as Yahoo!, Hotmail and Gmail. Outlook has a more sophisticated product, but requires purchase of a license. Even more sophisticated systems are available as stand-alone products. And, of course, very sophisticated systems are integrated into most CMS (case management software). The ABA Legal Technology Resource Center, http://www.abanet.org/tech/ltrc/home.html, contains a fairly comprehensive list of software solutions for most office systems. Be aware that not all software calendars are suitable for law office use, particularly those that come with word processing software.

In most cases, your office will have a software system already in place. You can be helpful in assessing the usefulness of that system in the context of the work you and others in the office do. However, it is likely that your only involvement, at least initially, will be in the use of the existing system.

Learn your office software calendar system well, and use it to the full extent of its capability. Keep in mind why *you are using it and concentrate on those features which assist in the three primary functions of a calendar docket system in every law office:*

1. Collaboration and coordination of schedules and deadlines;
2. Updating of schedules and deadlines; and
3. Tickling or warning of deadlines.

If your office system is not adequate for these functions, don't sit and complain about it. Research a better system and make the case for a change. Perhaps the necessary changes can be made by modifying the present system. If all else fails supplement the existing system. Remember, *do not ignore or neglect the office system.*

E. Ethical Considerations

Most state rules regulating attorney conduct contain provisions requiring that the attorney act with diligence or to avoid neglect of a client file. The ABA Model Rules include Rule 1.2, "A lawyer shall act with reasonable diligence and promptness in representing a client." The comment to the rule gives more substance, "A lawyer's work load must be controlled so that each matter can be handled competently." It also states,

> Perhaps no professional shortcoming is more widely resented than
> procrastination. A client's interests often can be adversely affected by
> the passage of time or the change of conditions; in extreme instances,
> as when a lawyer overlooks a statute of limitations, the client's legal po-

sition may be destroyed. Even when the client's interests are not affected in substance, however, unreasonable delay can cause a client needless anxiety and undermine confidence in the lawyer's trustworthiness.

As we've already discussed, an effective calendar/docketing system is essential to controlling performance of an attorney's workload and that of the attorney's paralegal. Without such a system, including the tickler, deadlines such as statutes of limitations are very likely to pass. While every person in the legal team has some responsibility for making the calendar system work, only *you* can make sure your responsibility is met. You also have the responsibility for making sure the attorney's responsibility is met.

While there are many causes for ethical complaints against attorneys, few are as certain to generate a complaint as missing a deadline. Remember, however, that the rules do not stop at missed deadlines. Rather, the work load must be controlled so that each matter is handled competency. Amanda, Hank and Todd are far less likely to handle all the items on their workloads competently in the scenario described at the beginning of this chapter than they are with well-managed calendars.

In addition to the danger of stepping over an ethical boundary, an ineffective calendar system creates continuous malpractice traps. Missing a deadline that could have been met *is* malpractice. In fact, unlike some other malpractice claims, it is an easy malpractice claim to prove. Therefore, the time and expense necessary to maintain an effective calendar system pales in comparison to the time and expense of defending ethical complaints and malpractice complaints.

Conclusion

In this chapter we applied to docket or calendar management the same principles we applied in Chapters One and Two to managing your time and workload. As we progress you will see that the same principles can, and should, be applied to almost every aspect of paralegal practice. The key is to identify, analyze, prioritize, organize and then implement procedures or use techniques that allow you to manage rather than be managed.

Take a break and go check out your office calendar-docket-tickler system before going on to the next chapter. Make special note of how it handles the three primary functions essential to a law office system. Start thinking about how it could function better and how you can use it better.

Fortunately there are ways to avoid both the ethical complaints and malpractice claims based on missed deadlines and *YOU know them. Use them.*

Chapter Four

Managing Your Files— I Know I Have That Here Somewhere!

The Client File is the lynch pin of every legal matter handled by your office. The effective, empowered paralegal manages files well. The best crafted deeds, contracts, wills and pleadings are worthless if they cannot be found when needed. None of them can even be created if the necessary information cannot be located in a timely manner, or was never obtained in the first place. It is essential that both the paralegal and the attorney have a system in place, and use that system, for organizing, identifying, indexing and tracking files and the materials contained in the files.

The professional paralegal has and uses the ability to locate a document or piece of information from a file quickly and accurately. The ability to do this depends upon the system in place to store and save documents and information in a case. Nina Platt is credited with saying, "Case management = knowledge management = the creation of a system or process in an environment that allows all employees to have access to information they need to develop the knowledge to do their jobs."[1]

The good news is that most offices already have a system in place for doing these things. If your office does not, then your first order of business should be to establish one. Fortunately, this chapter will be short since the tools you learned in the first three chapters are the same tools you will need to establish a system for files in your office. Identify the issues that need to addressed, analysis each issue to determine where it is being handled efficiently and effectively, and where it is not, then develop and put into place a well-ordered system for dealing with those impediments

---

1. Quoted in "The Unnatural Practice of Case Management" http://lnhostedservices.com/ Powerpoint/LawyersEast/Unnatural_Practice_of_Case_Management.ppt#284, 1, The Unnatural Practice of Case Management.

The first step is to identify what is needed and what the impediments are to meeting those needs. Here, we have already established that files need to be identified, organized, indexed and tracked. We will briefly look at each of these. Ultimately the answer is an office-wide system. In many respects it is less important what that system is than that there be a system. The chapter will end with a discussion of case management software.

A. The Essentials of Managing Files

The case file may be one manila folder or several such folders in a larger red, expanding envelop. It may include notebooks for depositions, closings, corporate records, and trials. Regardless of the format of the case file, each aspect of it must be identified, organized, indexed and tracked. Your system should be set up so that at anytime you can locate the file and any particular document or exhibit associated with that file quickly. At the same time you should be able to look at any document and associate it with the proper file without difficulty.

Identifying

Some offices identify a file simply by labeling it with the client's name, the case number, date of occurrence, attorney and paralegal assigned to the file and other pertinent information. This method raises issues of confidentiality. Take the case of a juvenile accused of a crime. Even the identity of the juvenile is supposed to remain confidential by law. Yet, the attorney may be in the position of walking around the court house or other locations with a file that clearly and openly states to the public the juvenile's name and the fact that he is a defendant in a court action! In addition, since this information is usually typed onto a file tab, it can make locating a particular file in full drawer or on a shelf full of files difficult.

The better procedure is to determine what information is necessary for file identification in your office. Generally you will want to be able to look at a file and tell (1) who the client is, (2) what type of case it is, (3) what attorney is assigned to it, (4) what paralegal is handling it and (4) some significant date, for example, the statute of limitations. Other information may also be desirable depending on the size of your office and the nature of the work your office does. Some information may not be necessary. In a one attorney office it is clear which attorney is handling the file. If you office handles only workers compensation claim, there is no need to identify the type of case.

Most of this information can be handled through color coded folders, labels and tags—A blue folder for personal injury cases, a red label for attorney Jones with a second green tab for paralegal O'Reilly, and so on. Client information can be handled through initials or partial names. Often this type of coding can be combined with tags such as that shown to the right here. This type of tag can be obtained in multiple colors for additional coding.

Which colors are used to indicate which information may depend on how your office separates files for access in your office. In some offices files are separated by type, i.e., all personal injury cases in one area, all criminal cases in another and so on. In others they are separated by the attorney handling them. In still others, they are stored chronologically. If all of attorney Martinez's files are stored right outside his door in one group, then it may be best for the most prominent color to be the one that indicates which paralegal is assigned to the case. If all files are stored in one file room, then the most prominent color may identify which attorney is associated with the file.

Each office should establish a method of identifying files that works well for that office. Once that method is established it must be used consistently office-wide. There will always be some members of the staff—perhaps you— who have a better method or at least a method that works better for them. However, in order for a system to work, consistency is an absolute necessity. In this instance, individual creativity must be sacrificed for the benefit of the system provided to the overall office. If you have great ideas for improving the system, bring them to the attention of your attorney or the office manager. If they are accepted, they can be made part of the master system and used consistently be everyone. If they are not, do not implement them independently.

Organization

Files also require a system of internal organization that is implemented across the office. The system may be as simple as all correspondence on the left and all pleadings on the right secured chronologically. There may be different systems for different types of cases. For example a personal injury case will require a method for storing and providing easy access to medical records, but a criminal defense case will not.

The system should be designed to provide for easy location of and access to those documents that are most likely to be accessed. One office with which I am familiar hole-punches all medical records and secures them to one side of the file, but overlays other documents on top of the medical records. This means every time new medical records come in or the existing records need to be copied for an insurance adjuster, expert, evaluator, etc., many unrelated documents must be removed and then replaced by lining up the holes in the documents and sliding them over the fasteners. This wastes time and increases the chances of the other documents being lost or misfiled. Since repeated access to the medical records is likely to be necessary, the system should place them on top or in a separate folder for easy access.

Separate documents by type and arrange them consistently from file to file. For example, you might keep all correspondence together, all motions together, all pleadings together, all documents relating to accident reconstruction together, and so on. Label each section. Within each section have a consistent organizational method. Correspondence may be arranged chronologically, medical records by service provider and each provider's records chronologically.

Include a method for tracking documents not in the file. There should be a form available for insertion in the file at the spot from which a document is taken showing who has the document, where it can be found and the purpose of removal. If a set of medical records is sent to the copy room for duplication, the form would indicate that paralegal Collier removed the records and gave them to the copy clerk for duplication and mailing to adjuster Wassermann on January 20th.

Sequester original exhibits. That crucial affidavit loses some of its luster when it is accidentally written upon by the attorney or paralegal. Make a working copy to include in the main file. Provide a method for tracking the originals and associating them with the file.

Indexing

Indexing is essential for any file of substance and should be used even for small files to maintain a uniform system. If it is used with all files, it will soon become a habit for the entire staff. Indexing can be as simple as a table of contents. The top document on the left hand side of the file may be a list of the documents on that side. Let's say you have the pleadings in a case arranged chronologically from the beginning of the case on the bottom to the most current on top. Separate the documents with alphabetically tabbed separators. Your table of contents or index might read:

A. Complaint
B. Motion to Dismiss
C. Objection to Motion to Dismiss
D. Order on Motion to Dismiss

E. Answer and Counterclaim

F. Reply to Counterclaim

G. Scheduling Order

At times the indexing may be more complex. If important information is contained in particular medical documents, you may add a reference to that information to the location of those documents on your table of contents.

Tracking

Your case file system should provide a method for tracking files as well as the contents of those files as discussed above. Include a method for associating individual manila folders and notebooks with their case file. For example, each could contain the same color/alphanumeric coding as the main file.

Use space holder forms for files removed from drawer or shelf storage. The form should indicate the date the file was removed, the person who removed it, where the file can be found and when it is expected to be returned. In effect, the system should act like a library system for checking out and return of books.

B. Case Management Software

While the client file is the lynch pin of every legal matter handled by your office, every paralegal knows managing the file is only a small part of case management. Case management includes managing the calendar/docket, evidence, exhibits, timekeeping, billing, communications and even clients. In the best of law offices, case management can be overwhelming and the brunt of case management falls on the paralegal. Fear not—there are solutions.

As we discussed in the last chapter, there are software technology solutions to any problem except the problem of paying for the software technology. (Although an argument can be made—and you may want to make it in encouraging your office to eliminate or shorten tasks as we discussed in Chapter One —that any software of real substance and value will save more than it costs.) There are a variety of case management solutions. Some focus on one aspect of the case management bundle. For example there are many possible software solutions to calendar and docket control. We will take a look at some of those solutions below for purposes of illustration. Others, referred to as case management systems or case management software, provide a fully integrated set of solutions covering most, if not, all aspects of case management. The trick is finding the right solution. Then that solution has to be understood, implemented and utilized.

Why a Software Solution?

Do we need a software solution? After all, law offices have managed cases with paper for decades. While this is true, it is also true that law offices used carbon paper to make copies and typewriters to type pleadings for decades! In fact, law offices once operated without paralegals. Clearly that is not a time to which we want to return.

It is not just that there are problems with paper case management systems. For example, any decent calendar control system requires several paper compilations. Even in a one attorney/one paralegal office there's a calendar for your attorney, one for the office and one for you, plus the tickler. Keeping them updated and correlated is a significant project requiring a substantial expenditure of time. When you are done with them, you have to store them, using more time and often valuable space. There may be value in having at least one paper calendar, especially one posted where all relevant personnel can see it without booting up the computer, but paper calendars simply cannot provide the synchronization, integration, portability and accessibility provided by calendar software.

Software Solution Options

As was the case with calendar management software, there are fairly inexpensive (and sometimes free) options for each aspect of case management and for case management as a whole. Calendar management is only one part of total case management. Similar stand-alone products are available for many aspects of case management. However, one primary value of software is the ability to provide synchronization, integration and collaboration. Comprehensive case management software provides solutions for each case management task in a synchronized, integrated and collaborative environment, not only within the individual task (calendar control, document control, client information, etc.), but in the total case management environment.

Let's consider what case management software does. Any case management software company will give you a list of the features contained in management of the case. For example, AmicusAttorney[2] lists:

---

2. Reference to AmicusAttorney is made for purposes of illustration only. It is not an endorsement of this product over other software solution products.

Track matters/cases in files

File chronology

Create and re-use precedents

Calendar with appointments, to-dos, tasks, milestone dates and deadlines

Group scheduling and group schedule printouts

Conflict of Interest checking

DO™ button intelligent assistance

Create time entries automatically from events, phone calls, emails and library research

Time entry statistics

Contact management

Full text document management

Palm® OS Synchronization

Legal research and knowledge management

Auto-dial with modem

Document assembly

Secondary Office—work at home or on the road

ComCenter telephone and email message management

Over 50 pre-defined reports

Outlook contact & calendar link

Tutorials and example database

But a list of features does not convey the importance of the system to the paralegal or the law office. In the end it is all about knowledge and information.

The professional paralegal has the ability to understand what information is necessary and the knowledge to use that information when it is retrieved. The biggest obstacle the paralegal has to performing his job is being able to access, locate and retrieve that information in a timely and useable fashion. Case management software *when correctly implemented and used* removes that obstacle.

The real reason to move on from a paper based system lies in the ability of case management software to allow lawyers and paralegals to be very good at what they do by removing the biggest roadblock to doing their jobs effectively. The best attorney cannot effectively use an affidavit to cross examine a witness if the affidavit cannot be located and related to the witness and the facts of the case when it is needed. We will consider the importance of this ability to relate various aspects of a case in detail in Chapter 7, Managing Your Litigation

Removing that roadblock has corollary benefits: it makes the legal team look good to their clients, and lessens the chance of malpractice and ethical violations. Ross L. Kodner notes the following the information managed by case management software:

- Case information about each of your matters—everything including party contact info, counsel, courts, experts, witnesses and tracking fact patterns, issues and case strategies.
- Calendaring, docketing and tickler systems as well as to-do list managers.
- Conflict of interest searches—light years ahead of the time-tested but terrifying method used by many firms where a lawyer sticks their head out of their office and shouts down the hall "Yoohoo! Has anyone ever heard of so and so?"
- Case notes, logged as you work your files—instead of endlessly proliferating sticky notes.
- Emails and documents related to your cases—a centralizing source for all work product coming into the firm or flowing out.
- Firm administrative information—as important as tracking client-related matters since every firm's single most important client is … itself!
- Custom information for document assembly—the vast array of information tracked and stored by a case manager can be extracted and flowed into documents.[3]

All this information is portable, that is, it can be accessed via laptop, Palm or Pocket PC and similar means. It can be accessed by everyone in the firm from anywhere and at any time. (This should mean no more calls at your home from your attorney wondering where to find the list of medical bills for the Jones case.) All the information is stored and tracked in a searchable database. It can generally be compiled in a manner useable for the purpose for which it is needed and printed when desired.

Case Management Software Cautions

Now a word or two of caution: There are dangers in the use of any technology. Case management software is no different. Dangers include:

- The information stored in, managed by, and retrieved from a case management system is only as reliable as the information that is entered into the system. For example, an important date entered into the system is entered into *everyone's* calendar incorrectly. There remains no substitute for double-checking and verification of data. All information entered should be reviewed by at least two people.

---

3. Ross L. Kodner, *Features—Case Management Systems: Practical Tips for Implementation Success*, Published on March 18, 2002, http://www.llrx.com/features/cmsystems.htm. Retrieved September 29, 2008.

- The ease of use of several of the subsystems can lead to information over-load. Anyone who suffers that Monday Morning Migraine in anticipation of opening their email Inbox has experienced this problem.
- With case management software information is available from anywhere and at any time. I already noted this as an advantage, but it is also a danger if you become psychologically attached to your Blackberry.
- All software systems that provide for access to your CPU or the office server create a security risk. In addition, there is constant potential for breaches of confidentiality when information is transferred over the Internet.
- The information you enter is accessible to everyone and recorded for-ever, including those not-so-nice comments you have made about clients, opposing counsel, court clerks and judges. In most systems when you send an email to your attorney it is posted automatically to the client's file and remains there for all with access to see.

This merits further discussion and an illustrative example. Case manage-ment software is not a solution to a problem if all you do is transfer the prob-lem, that is, if you simply move the mess you used to have on your desk into the computer. Computers can not organize chaos especially when the people entering information into the computer are the same ones who created the chaos. People who work at the information technology help desk often make the following entry on their report of a call and its resolution: PEBKAC which stands for "Problem Exists Between Chair and Keyboard."

Making a system work, even a computer software system, is all about the de-tails, and you provide the details. Let's take a look at the illustrative example. On October 8, 2008, Shannon Duffy posted the story of Attorney Brian M. Puricelli on www.law.com. After winning a jury verdict Puricelli filed a peti-tion for more than $180,000 in attorney fees that was riddled with typographical and other sorts of errors. The sloppy pleading clearly angered the judge who spent the first three pages of his opinion just describing the errors, adding "[sic]" after each one, and ultimately slashed the fees to about $26,000.

According to Duffy, among the many misspellings flagged by Ditter were "plaintf," "Philadehia," "attoreys," "reasonbale" and "Ubited States." Puricelli also wrote the phrase "mocong papers" where he clearly intended to write "moving papers." And in the proposed order attached to the motion, Puricelli had evi-dently *cut and pasted* from a document in a different case without changing the defendants' names or the dollar figures,[4] leading Ditter to say, "It is suggested

---

4. This is a constant problem with the use of computer stored form and document banks. Such devices are invaluable to the modern law office, but they are also an invitation

that I sign an order which recites the wrong amount of McKenna's judgment and orders three strangers to this action to pay attorneys' fees and costs." Puricelli explained that his original filing, which he agreed was riddled with typos, was the result of a filing error. Using the court's electronic filing system, he said, he had accidentally filed a "draft" version that had not been proofread.

These sorts of problems with the utilization of software can be managed and avoided. Keep the following in mind:

- Document management technology does not replace sound document management PRACTICES.
- Be aware of the relationship between the document management technology and the real life documents
- View document management as a part of total case management
- KNOW your practices AND your technology

Case Management Software Systems

Case management software systems have proliferated in the last decade. This forum cannot review them all. The ABA Legal Technology Resource Center, http://www.abanet.org/tech/ltrc/home.html, contains a fairly comprehensive list of software solutions for most office systems. There are two basic types of systems—those designed for use in a general practice and those designed for specific types of practices such personal injury, bankruptcy, immigration, social security disability and the like. There is even a system designed for a public defender's office. Many of the companies marketing general practice software also sell "special editions" for specific practice areas. URLs for some of the more popular systems are provided at the end of this discussion. This listing should not be taken as an endorsement for any of the systems listed.

Your Role

As was discussed in the chapter on docket and calendar control, in most cases your office will already have a software system in place. You can be helpful in assessing the usefulness of that system in the context of the work you and others in the office do. However, it is likely that your only involvement, at least initially, will be in the use of the existing system. *Learn your office system*

---

to laziness and a trap for those who use them in a hurry. Each client is unique. You cannot just buy a dress or suit off the rack for a client and you cannot *just* take a Will off the form rack for a client. "Cut and paste" is not a substitute for "think and write."

software well, and use it to the full extent of its capability. Keep in mind *why* you are using it: it allows you to be the professional you are and empowers you to do your job effectively by providing timely access to synchronized and integrated information on all aspects of your client's case.

Links to Case Management Software Sites

General
> www.amicusattorney.com
> www.timematters.com
> www.abacuslaw.com
> www.easysoft-usa.com
> www.legalmaster.com
> www.needleslaw.com
> www.pclaw.com
> www.prolaw.com
> www.stilegal.com
> www.timeslips.com

Specialty
> www.bestcase.com (Bankruptcy)
> http://www.lawlogix.com/Law_Firm_Immigration_LLX.html (Immigration)
> http://www.personalinjurycopilot.com/?HURT911 (Personal Injury—Online)
> http://home.att.net/~crocodileconsulting1/ssd_main_switchboard.htm (Social Security Disability
> http://www.abacuslaw.com/products/specialeditions/familylaw.html (Family Law)

C. Ethical and Malpractice Considerations

As indicated in Chapter Three, most state rules regulating attorney conduct contain provisions requiring that the attorney act with diligence or to avoid neglect of a client file. Missing or misused documents are extremely likely to result in ethical complaints and malpractice claims. Just as an effective calendar/docketing system is essential to controlling performance on an attorney's workload and that of the attorney's paralegal, effective file and case management gives you and your attorney control over the information necessary for your office to avoid those complaints.

Therefore, the time and expense necessary to maintain effective file management pales in comparison to the time and expense of defending ethical complaints and malpractice complaints.

Conclusion

The professional paralegal has the ability to understand what information is necessary and the knowledge to use that information when it is retrieved. The biggest obstacle the paralegal has to performing his job is being able to access, locate and retrieve that information in a timely and useable fashion. Case management software when correctly implemented and used removes that obstacle. Removing that roadblock has corollary benefits: it makes the legal team look good to their clients, and lessens the chance of malpractice and ethical violations.

Remember these two important facts about information managed by case management software:

- The information stored in, managed by, and retrieved from a case management system is only as reliable as the information that is entered into the system. For example, an important date entered into the system is entered into everyone's calendar incorrectly. There remains no substitute for double-checking and verification of data. All information entered should be reviewed by at least two people.
- Those not-so-nice comments about the client you make in a memo to your attorney are available to everyone with access.

In addition, any software solution must be based on a real system in the office. Software cannot organize chaos.

The office system should be designed so that files and their contents are easy to locate and be used by those most likely to use them. Once the system is established, all persons should be trained in how to use it and how to locate documents within it. Everyone associated with the files should be directed to post documents to the file the day they come in with proper indexing. Everyone associated with the file should be instructed to re-post any documents removed from the file as soon as the document is not longer needed. Do not assume the system makes so much sense that it is self-evident how it is meant to be used. This may not be the case, especially for your attorney.

With a well-designed system used consistently and well, you can work professionally, effectively and efficiently. You and your legal team will look good because you will have quick and accurate access to all the information you need.

Speaking of the client, now that you are managing the basic non-human aspects of your job (time, workload, docket and files), it is time to tackle client management. When you are ready, take deep breath and turn to Chapter Five.

CHAPTER FIVE

MANAGING YOUR CLIENTS—MR. JONES IS ON THE LINE AGAIN!

The essence of people management in case management is the same as in most other circumstances—preparation, understanding, communication, clarity and organization. We will focus on the client since he is such an important member of the legal team, but many of the same principles and techniques apply to witnesses and other people with whom you will deal in any legal proceeding.

A. The Client as Part of the Legal Team

Our discussion starts where the introduction of this book starts—with an understanding of who the members of the legal team are and the role each member plays in relation to the legal matter being handled by the team. Before moving on, we'll do a quick review.

A diagram of the traditional concept of the legal team looks much like a corporation or government organizational chart with a rigid hierarchy of commands, responsibilities and duties (see Figure 5.1).

This traditional view of the legal team suffers from several flaws, the most prominent of which is that it fails to recognize the role of the client. The importance of the client to the law office is often recognized only to the extent of acknowledging that without the client there is no case and no fee. This results in a minor change to the chart (see Figure 5.2).

However, recognizing the importance of the client to the law office is not the same as recognizing the client as part of the legal team; rather it keeps the client apart from the team and, to a great extent, from the very legal matter which brought the client to the attorney. Effective management of the client in litigation and other legal processes requires that we change the conception of those roles from the traditional view to one such as that shown in this diagram (see Figure 5.3).

55

Figure 5.1

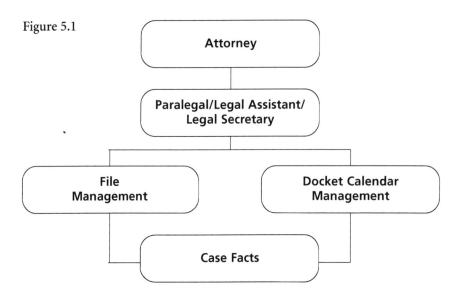

Figure 5.2

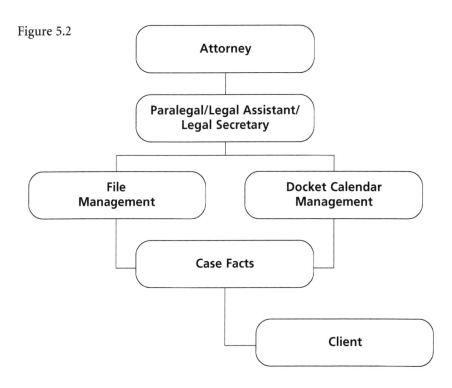

Figure 5.3

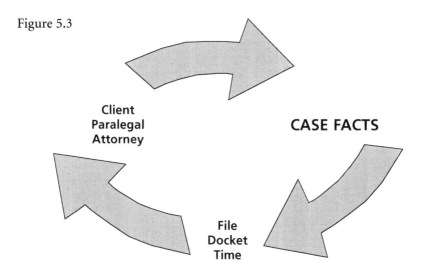

This diagram begins to account for these fundamental *inter*relationships and responsibilities:

- The interrelationship between the facts, the file, the docket and time
- The interrelationship between the client, the paralegal and the attorney
- The joint responsibility and involvement of all members of the legal team for the facts, the file and the docket in achieving a successful outcome.

These interrelationships and responsibilities appear more complex than they have often been characterized. The goal for the effective, empowered paralegal is the ability to understand and manage each of the key factors, including the client. When the client is a full-functioning member of the legal team, management of interrelated aspects of the legal process becomes much easier.

Let's consider what can happen when the client has not been made a member of the legal team:

NaShana wants nothing more than for this day to end. She and her attorney have just wasted an exhausting morning in a mediation that might better be described as a disaster. First, the client, Joan, did not show up on time, which was inexcusable since NaShana had sent her a letter stating the date, time and location of the mediation. When Joan did show up she appeared disheveled, dirty, groggy, disoriented and irritable. Even when alone with NaShana and her attorney, the client seemed confrontational. It was almost as if she did not understand that NaShana and the attorney were on her side. She certainly didn't understand the role of the mediator who she kept on demanding "rule in her favor." She got very upset every time the mediator said anything that questioned her position or suggested that she should consider weaknesses in her case. More than once, she implied that the mediator must be "in the other side's pocket." Joan's irritation grew every time the mediator met privately with the other side, especially when the meetings went for more than a few minutes. She was very impatient and kept looking at the clock. Well before the mediation was done, Joan insisted she could not stay longer and walked out, leaving NaShana's attorney to explain her sudden absence. If NaShana and the attorney has realized the client would be like this they never would have agreed to the mediation in the first place.

We all feel sorry for NaShana and many of us have been through mornings like hers. What I would like you to consider is that NaShana likely *could* have known the client would be like she was and avoided many of these problems. Indeed, the empowered paralegal makes it her responsibility to know, prepare for and avoid such occurrences. The empowered paralegal doesn't just have clients, she manages her clients. The effective legal team does not serve a client, it makes the client part of that team.

In order to "manage" the client we need to bring him on board as a member of the legal team. For the most part this can be done relatively simply— communicate with the client, explain the process to the client and explain the client's role in the process to the client. In an interview with Tom Friedman[1] at the National Press Club, Dov Seidman,[2] author of *How,* wonderfully explained this using business management terms in a way that can also apply to the client's role in the legal team.

Seidman uses The Wave that often occurs in sports stadiums full of fans to illustrate his point. Think of the first person to attempt a wave. How did he get it going? He did not turn to the person next to him and threaten him to get him to join in. Nor did he motivate the people who followed him with money, that is, by offering them each twenty dollars to stand up and wave their hands at the right moment. Certainly he did not get the cooperation he wanted by keeping his plan secret. That is, he did not turn to the folks next to him and say, "When I tell you, stand up and wave your hands, but I am not going to tell

---

1. *New York Times* columnist and author of *The World is Flat.*

2. Information regarding Dov Seidman, *How,* and the "Making Waves" interview is available at http://www.howsmatter.com/.

you why." In order to get their cooperation and the collaboration he, as Seidman puts it, "shared his vision."

All too often, we attempt to get our client's cooperation through coercion (If you don't get these answers into the court by Friday, the court may issue sanctions), or promises of monetary reward (If you do what we say, you are more likely to win a big judgment). For many clients neither of these will be sufficiently motivating if we keep the reasons why their cooperation is important secret. Our clients will assist us best if we make them part of the team by "sharing the vision," that is, by explaining to them what the legal process is for obtaining what they want (a successful outcome of their case, a smooth real estate closing, etc.) and their role in that process.

Every opportunity should be used to make the client part of the team, starting with the initial client interview and continuing through every substantive client contact.

B. Interviewing and Instructing the Client

In the day-to-day operation of the law office, the importance of the client interview is often forgotten. Certainly most offices make an effort to impress the client in order to obtain and retain business. We make the client, to the extent possible, feel comfortable. We also do our best to be attentive, empathetic and not to rushed, all while letting the client know just how important and busy the office is. In doing so, we can miss real opportunity presented by the client interview — the opportunity to make the client part of the legal team.

Bringing the client on board not just as a source of work and a fee, but as a member of the team during interviews and meetings can save the team a great deal of time, effort and frustration in all but the simplest of legal matters. It is during interviews that you can gain an understanding of the client, engage the client in the process, instruct the client, establish lines of communication, establish ground rules and set limits.

Many times the initial interview is limited to obtaining necessary information from the client and establishing the attorney/client relationship — setting the terms of employment and payment. We may go further and explain what the client can expect *of us*. However, the initial interview is an excellent opportunity to explain to the client what to expect *of the process*, whether it be litigation, a real estate closing, formation of a business, administration of an estate or other legal process, and what we expect *of them* over and above payment of our fee.

While most of what follows will be cast in terms of a formal, initial interview, the principles discussed apply to a greater or lesser degree to every substantial client contact.

Prepare for the Interview

The key to client management is the same as it is to managing your time, work load, docket calendar and files: assessment, preparation, organization and control. Seldom will you meet with a client with literally no idea regarding either who the client is, what the topic of the meeting is or both. Rarely does a client succeed in making an appointment on nothing more than the assertion that, "I just want to talk to an attorney."

If the client is a returning client, take a moment to recall who she is and why she has been in before. I recommend keeping a client data file that allows a quick way of refreshing your memory and the memory of your attorney. As discussed in previous chapters, this can now be accomplished easily with case management software, but it is not impossible or even difficult without such software. After all, shrewd businessmen and politicians did it for centuries before the advent of software.

Knowing your client provides benefits beyond simply being able to make them feel comfortable and feel wanted. It allows you to anticipate and make the most of the interview with a minimum of time. Perhaps you will need special seating arrangements because the client is hard of hearing, is morbidly obese or has a bad back. Perhaps the client is a visual learner and will need aids. This point may be easier to see in the context of the likely topics of interviews.

Generally you will have some idea of the topic of the interview — the client is considering a divorce, has been in a car accident, was just fired, wants to buy a house, is arguing with a neighbor over a boundary, has been arrested, etc. Anticipate what will be required to make the most out of the meeting:

- Unless the topic is one with which you deal daily, quickly review the law.
- Outline the information you are likely to need from the client. Develop a checklist or bring a standardized, topic-specific checklist with you if one is available. Interview forms can also be developed for specific topics. Some offices have a general information form for all client meetings supplemented by specific forms designed to get the information necessary for a particular legal proceeding. The information necessary for a divorce proceeding is quite different from that needed for a personal injury case that is in turn quite different from that needed for a real estate closing, and so on.

- Consider what visual aids might be helpful. For example, you may need a chart showing the standard path for civil litigation, or a list of documents needed to begin an estate administration.
- Anticipate documents it would be helpful for your client to sign, such as healthcare information releases or forms appointing your office as agent for purposes of the IRS.
- Consider whether it will be helpful to have pre-set diagrams or charts available for the client to use in explaining his problem to you. For example, in a personal injury case it is often helpful to have a diagram of the human form available for the client to show the nature and extent of injuries.
- Be prepared to dispel common misconceptions held by lay people about legal processes. For example, many clients will believe that there is no difference between facts, evidence and proof, a distinction we will discuss shortly in the next section. Many people believe that they have an open and shut case because there is an eyewitness, because they have no understanding of the vagrancies of eyewitnesses and the effects of cross examination.

Many of these preparations will be helpful regardless of the client, but to the extent you have previous experience with and knowledge of the client, you can maximize the benefits.

Explain the Basics to the Client

In order for the client to fulfill her role in the legal team she must have at least a basic understanding of the substantive and procedural law applicable to her legal matter. For example, in litigation most clients will start with some basic *mis*understandings about (1) evidence, (2) their cause of action, (3) their role in the litigation and (4) court procedure. Clients have similar misunderstanding about deeds and the real estate closing process, wills and the probate process, disability and the Social Security Disability claims process and so on. It will usually fall to the paralegal to correct these misconceptions. Often it will be necessary to explain each more than once in order to remove the misconceptions and instill the correct understanding.

It is not necessary to provide each client with a complete legal education. It is even possible to tell a client too much. The basics are all that is necessary. For example the basics of the distinction between facts, evidence and proof may include:

> *Facts* of a case are the bits and pieces that comprise what happened —the event which brought the parties to court; the particularities of the automobile accident, the assault, the boundary dispute, the con-

tract dispute and so on. For example, it may be a fact of an automobile accident case that one went through an intersection when the traffic light in his direction was red. However, this "fact" may be contested by the parties. One party may say the light was red and the other party may say it was green.

Evidence is something that tends to show, confirm or verify a fact. It can be testimony such as the driver testifying he looked at the light before he entered the intersection. Not all evidence is equally convincing. Testimony from an un-involved third party, i.e., a school crossing guard, that the light was red or green, may be more convincing than the testimony of the driver of either car involved in the accident. A picture taken by a camera set up to track drivers' speed may be even more convincing.

From the lawyer's perspective evidence is more important than actual facts. Cases must be evaluated and presented based on the evidence available for presentation rather than on the facts the attorney believes is true. We are more concerned about what can be proven than simply what occurred. We can assure our clients that we believe the doctor told them they would never be the same, but must make them understand that what matters is what the doctor says in his reports and on the witness stand.

Proof is simply whatever evidence is sufficient to convince a jury to accept a fact as true. Thus, a driver's testimony that the light was green when she went through the intersection is proof if it is credible enough for the jury to accept it as a true statement of the facts; it is not proof if the jury does not accept it.

Written Informational Forms

It is helpful to have standard pre-prepared written explanations in the form of brochures, checklists, instructions or letters. Your office should have an ample and easily accessible collection of relevant instructional materials written in "plain language" in a system designed to ensure their delivery to the client at each step in the process. However, not all clients have the same capacity or motivation to read or comprehend such aids.

Clients are, after all, people and each person learns differently—some learn better through reading, but many learn best through hearing, visual aids or physical activity, i.e., walking through the process. Some clients do not read well (or at all) but will be reluctant to reveal this fact. Many clients will not realize the importance of reading and following written instructions.

Many will read them with their own pre-conceptions or understanding of words which differ dramatically from the legal perspective from which they were written.

Communicating Understanding

Ultimately, the lawyer and you are responsible for knowing each client well enough to understand how best to not only communicate *with* the client but to communicate an understanding of the essentials *to* that client.

Start during your initial interview with the client:

- Establish the best physical method(s) of communicating with the client (phone, email, mail) as well as the best times to attempt that communication.
- In addition to oral explanations, use diagrams and walk them through some written instructions.
- Watch the client's body language, especially their eyes and face, for signs of understanding or confusion.
- Ask questions designed to ascertain whether the client understands what you or the attorney has said.
- Be aware that clients are often reluctant to discuss personal matters, even though they made the appointment for that purpose. They may want to get a divorce because their spouse cheated on them with the babysitter, but that does not mean they want to talk about it. Be patient. Assure them you understand. Explain why you need the information. Remind them that what they tell you will remain confidential.
- Be aware that clients do not know what you need to know. Some will be all too ready to talk, but will talk for quite some time without touching upon what you need. They do not know the elements of the cause of action. You do, so it up to you to ask. Explain to them what you need to know and why you need to know it.
- Be aware that the client does not understand terms that we take for granted, and many, if not most, will not want to ask what those terms mean. It is not likely you will get a full and helpful response to the question, "Are there any un-filed mechanic's liens on the property?" unless you either explain what a mechanic's lien is and how they arise or put the question in terms they can understand. Try, "Has anyone done any work on the property, made any improvements to the property or delivered to or installed on the property items such as water heaters, furnaces or cabinets within the last ninety days?"

Begin Client Management

This also the best time to initiate client management. Make it clear your office represents many clients and you have a system for seeing that each case is treated with the utmost of professional care. When you and the attorney are working on that client's case, it (and they) will receive undivided attention. In turn, when you or the attorney are working on another client's case, it must also receive undivided attention. Remember this means you cannot take calls or allow other interruptions when you are interviewing the client!

While establishing means for communication *to* the client, explain your office procedures for communications *from* the client. For example, explain when the client *must* communicate with you, e.g., if he is contacted by an adjuster or investigator, if there is a change in her medical condition or simply once a week at a set time. Explain when to expect responses from you or the attorney to calls or other communications, e.g., within twenty-four hours, only between 2:00 and 4:00 p.m. You should also explain when a client should acknowledge communications from you.

Do Not Assume Understanding

In general it is best not to assume that your client understands *anything*, including the importance of meeting deadlines and following through on commitments. In most cases it simply is not enough to explain to a client, for example, what interrogatories are and that they must be answered within thirty days. You will also need to explain to them what that means in terms of the overall scheduling of the timely completion of the answers. In order for you and the attorney to draft, review, correct, revise and fill in gaps in the answers, the client must get initial information to you by a date far short of the thirty days. Set dates for completion of each task the client must complete.

It is human nature to delay unpleasant tasks. It is likely that left on their own the clients will treat each deadline as many treat filing taxes. Just as many people rush to the tax preparer on April 14th with a shoebox full of receipts and tax forms, clients will wait until day twenty-nine to start answering interrogatories due on day thirty. When you meet with the client to explain the interrogatories, give them an instruction sheet that repeats your explanation and instructions, including the specific dates for completion of any task you assign to them. Write this information down for them before they leave. Again, your office may have or you can develop standardized checklists or forms for this purpose. (Some clients may protest that they came to you to do the work and do not understand why they have to do so much. This can be avoided by a clear explanation during the initial interview with appropriate reminders during the process that they are an essential part of the litigation team with their own role to fill.)

Once the client leaves, immediately enter the date for *your* follow-up reminders to the client on your calendar. Do not assume the client is out there somewhere faithfully doing exactly what you told them to do. Send a reminder in writing and set a date for a follow up telephone call. If you send an email or leave a voicemail message, ask that they respond with an update on the status of their progress so you know they got the message and can make a file note. This seems like a lot work, but much of it can be systematized and it serves several functions:

- It makes the client aware of how important they are to the litigation process;
- It makes the client aware of how much attention your office is paying to them and their case;
- It provides a record in the event the client later claims your office "dropped the ball"; and
- It is likely to be less work than that required to obtain extensions of time or to avoid sanctions from the court.

Prepare the Client

Preparing the client for depositions, trials, a real estate closing or a mediation session requires more than just reviewing their testimony or telling them to show up on time. Most clients never will have been through a closing or the litigation process, much less been the star of a trial presentation. Explain the process to them. Let them know who else will be participating and what the role of each will be. Make it clear what is expected of them. Give them a checklist of items they should bring or do. If appropriate, tell him how to dress.

Exactly what should be done to prepare the client depends on the legal event in which she will be involved and the client herself. For example, preparing a client for a court proceeding my include bringing him to the courthouse and the courtroom in advance. A short trip to the courtroom in advance can change a client's entire attitude. Since he does not have to worry and wonder about details such as where he is going to sit, he can focus on his role, his testimony and the overall presentation. He may actually become helpful to the process, but at least he will not require as much of your attention during the trial. The same, to a degree, can be said of any legal matter from a simple Last Will and Testament execution to a closing of a complex corporate merger. This is not a one-size fits all task. It is your role to find the right size for the client.

Be Professional

We will discuss professionalism in some detail in Chapter Six. Many of the comments made there are applicable here, especially those regarding appearance and attitude. Right now, however, we will focus on some aspects of professionalism that are particularly directed towards managing the client. Some aspects of professionalism fall within the realms of preparation, organization and the information already covered in this and other chapters. Others include the following:

- Explain your role as a member of the legal team. Make it clear what you add to the legal team, but also make it clear what your limitations are. You want the client to understand how valuable you are and what important things you do, that is, what a professional you are, but you can best convey that message by *being professional* as discussed here and in Chapter Six. This is not the time to satisfy your own ego. Rather it is a time to inform the client. Overselling yourself can result in unreasonable expectations from the client who may then become frustrated and angry when you cannot answer a question or give advice so they have to wait until the attorney can respond. In addition, a client who is over-sold on a paralegal's capability may soon start to wonder why they are paying lawyer's rates when, in their mind, the paralegal could handle their work. As we discuss in Chapter Six, there is some confusion even within the legal profession regarding the role of the paralegal. The client will likely come to you as a clean slate in this regard. This is your opportunity to draw a sharp, clear, and pleasing picture on that slate.
- Leave your biases behind. Everyone has biases and it can be quite difficult to separate ourselves from those biases. We can not remove or eliminate the biases. However, as professionals we can separate ourselves from them. Indeed, we must separate ourselves from them if we are to do our jobs effectively. It is our role as professionals to be objective.
- This means we must avoid judging our client and our client's desires. For the attorney this frequently means doing what the client wants even when the attorney feels it is not in the client's best interest or even is not "the right things to do." (Although the smart attorney will create a written record that he has properly advised the client.) For example, the client may want to write her children out of her will and leave her fortune to the care of her dog. We may find this odd. It is not what we would do. We might not believe it is right.

It is the lawyer's role, however, to advise the client, not necessarily to persuade her. The attorney, and you, may take steps to make sure the client is truly competent to make testamentary decisions (and record those steps in the client file). The attorney will want to make sure the client understands the ramifications of what she is doing. But, in the end, if the client desires that disposition of her wealth, the attorney's, and your, job is to see that it happens, not to judge the wisdom of the decision.

- It is likely that you will be the primary contact with the client, so it is especially important that you not allow your biases to color your attitude towards the client, your communication with the client, your objective statement of the client's desires and the facts surrounding those desires in your reports to the attorney.
- Empathize with the client, but do not become attached or involved with the client on a personal basis. This is akin to the concern about biases coloring your ability to remain objective.
- Clients are people and people have faults. They can be whiny, rude, untruthful, critical, and all those other things we hate. They can react out of nervousness, stress and anxiety. You and your attorney are professionals and must "filter out" such irritants within reason. Respond to such clients professionally, not out of emotion. This is not to say you must tolerate excessive rudeness or any abuse. It is entirely proper to set limits. Discuss any such problems with your attorney as soon as they arise. Develop a plan for handling them on a professional basis.
- Use professional communication skills and listening skills.
  - Speak professionally.
  - Avoid slang.
  - Think before you speak.
  - Speak clearly.
  - Avoid mumbling, slurring of words and the like.
  - Pronounce words correctly.
  - Look at the client when you are speaking to her or she is speaking to you. Make eye contact to ensure she is paying attention and understanding.
  - Ask questions to clarify anything that seems unclear to you.
  - Ask yourself whether what you heard could be interpreted more than one way and then take measures to ensure you have interpreted it correctly.
  - Pay attention to body language.
  - Avoid interrupting the client, but be aware that you must control and direct the conversation so that it stays on point and addresses the specific information you and the attorney will need to do your jobs.

  ◦ Watch for signs of drugs, alcohol or mental disturbance, including stress that may impede understanding on the part of the client.

Ending the Interview

End the interview on a positive note. The client should be aware of how happy you and your attorney are to be working with her (as opposed to "for" her). Give her homework, that is, give her clear instructions as to what she should do and expect next. For example, write out for her that she needs to provide you with the names and addresses of each of the doctors that treated her for her personal injuries within one week on a form you have provided.

Do not give guarantees or promises regarding time frames on your end. If you think you will take ten days to obtain information from other sources, set a time frame of two weeks and advise it may take longer. It is better to pleasantly surprise a client by getting work done more quickly than expected, than to run late. Not only does the latter create bad feelings on their part, it also affects your credibility when you are insisting that they meet deadlines.

C. Understanding the Client

In the last section we talked extensively about getting the client to understand you. It is equally important to understand the client. Note that this isn't a matter of "understanding clients." Each client must be understood on their own. This means you have to get to know something about your client. What you need to know varies substantially depending on what services you are performing for the client. So we will mainly discuss this topic in a general way using examples along the way to illustrate how those generalities might apply to particular situations.

Barriers to Understanding

It is helpful to begin by considering some of the barriers to understanding. Some of the more common barriers arise from the differences that exist between humans. For example, we differ linguistically and educationally. We differ by class and culture, as well as personality, ethnicity and religion. Perhaps the best known exposition of differences is that regarding gender illustrated by John Gray in his book *Men Are from Mars, Women Are from Venus*.[3] For the most part, I

---

3. Published by HarperCollins (1993).

prefer to focus on our similarities rather than our differences. However, understanding differences and the way they act as barriers to effective communication and understanding of our clients can help us overcome those barriers.

Linguistic Barriers

The most frequent example of linguistic differences that interfere with understanding is generational. Every generation develops its own slang, leading to countless repetitions of basically the same joke about the inability of adults to understand their teenage children in generation after generation of family-based sitcoms since the beginning of television. Such differences can, in fact, cause real problems for understanding. They are not limited to generations. People with different educational, class, ethnic and cultural backgrounds can use terms differently.

Besides the misunderstanding that may result from the different meaning given by various speakers using the same terms, some may view certain terms as offensive while others do not. Obviously, when someone is offended by the language another person is using to express themselves, he is less likely to actually listen and understand what the offending person is saying. Currently many younger people have a different view on the use of "vulgar" language than was formerly considered acceptable. As professionals, we should be conscious of how such language affects us and move beyond it to gain an understanding of what our client is saying uncolored by the off-color language they are using. (The same is true in general—we have to move beyond our dislike of the client regardless of the source of the dislike and do our best for the client.)

While we are professionals, we are also people. There are times when language becomes so offensive to us that we can not simply move beyond it, especially language laced with racial, ethnic, gender or other pejorative connotations. When this happens you should discuss it with you attorney. It may be necessary for the attorney to take steps to control such a client. It is not your role to either tolerate such treatment or reprimand the client for it.

A second linguistic barrier arises from your status as a member of the legal profession. The legal profession has its own jargon. We use terms like "writ," "burden of proof" and "quit-claim deed." You already know that you must explain such terms to the client. Another problem arises, however, because clients hear these terms from friends, relatives and television, and use them. They believe that they know what they mean, which can at times make your job difficult because they are less likely to listen to you attentively when you try to explain what they really mean. In addition, because they use the terms and seem to have an understanding of them, you may be led to believe the client knows more than they really do. Again, you may find yourself speaking at cross-purposes because you have a different understanding of what a word means, even though you are both using the same word.

Be aware that clients may be hesitant to admit that they do not know the meaning of words that we consider part of everyday usage, even when they are not legal jargon. I have even found that many clients have managed to flourish in jobs that seem to require the ability to read even though they cannot! They are embarrassed to admit this type of inability and (understandably) will go to great lengths to avoid the issue. However, it is essential that we know such things about our clients. While it may work for the client to say to *us*, "Oh, I don't need to read it, I trust you," or "I left my glasses at home, will you read it to me," it could be a real problem if they are on the witness stand and decide to bluff their way through a request by opposing counsel to read a portion of an affidavit they signed!

We, of course, should do our best to maintain a relationship with our clients such that they will not feel embarrassed by revealing such limitations. Since not all clients will feel that comfortable with their attorney or paralegal, we should watch for signs and take steps to overcome these barriers. Since you are likely to have the most contact with the client, you will have the greatest opportunity to notice those signs.

Cultural and Other Barriers

Differences in culture, class, education and the like can affect not only how we speak and use particular words, but how we perceive the world, how we think, how we react to events, and how willing we are to talk about our real concerns. This can be as simple as the male personal injury client who thinks it "unmanly" to talk about his pain when we need him to explain it well during his deposition, or the previously discussed client who does not want to reveal that he cannot read.

I recall hearing of an experiment that illustrates the point well. It may be apocryphal, but it works, so we'll use it. In this experiment people from the United States, Europe and South Korea we asked the following hypothetical:

> You are a passenger in a friend's car. He is driving too fast and hits someone. The police are called and ask you whether your friend was speeding. Do you tell the truth?

A large number of Americans said they would tell the truth, a lesser number of Europeans and a very small number of Koreans. The really interesting part occurred in the next step. The Americans were told about the Korean results. Their reaction was basically that the Koreans had no ethical values because they did not respect truth. One the other hand, Koreans told of the American results stated that the Americans had no ethical values because they had no respect for friendship and loyalty.

As another example, I had a class for students who were trying to move from positions as "on the street" police officers to administrative positions—captains and eventually chiefs of police. We were discussing how to motivate police officers. Everyone student listed promotion as the primary motivator. Yet many people do not want the stress, responsibility, physical inactivity and isolation that come with those positions. Many would prefer to be in the community working with the citizens. The students had mistakenly assumed that everyone was motivated by the same thing that motivated them.

Factors that influence the way a client perceives and processes information they receive, and therefore influence their understanding of that information, include their education (the level of education, what the primary focus of that education was and sometimes where they were educated), their past experiences, their intelligences, their learning styles and their needs. We will discuss learning styles and needs later in this chapter. This section will end by noting that the word "intelligences" as used above is not a typographical error.

We generally speak of someone being intelligent, or not so intelligent, as if it were one unified concept that can be measured using just one measuring stick such as an "IQ" test. In 1983 Harvard Professor Howard Gardner published a theory contending that people should more properly be considered to have "intelligences," since they have several distinct cognitive abilities.[4] Each individual possesses each of these cognitive abilities in differing degrees. These cognitive abilities include logical or mathematical intelligence, linguistic intelligence, body intelligence (good athletes possess this), musical intelligence and spatial intelligence. Those of us with very good linguistic intelligence may consider a concept clear that is quite perplexing to a person whose chief intelligence is mathematical or musical.

Gardner's theory can be complex and has generate a good deal of commentary. We need not have an comprehensive understanding of the theory for its general concepts to be helpful to us. We will be discussing other ways in which people differ in understanding and approach. In no case are you expected to be an expert and be able to make a "diagnosis" regarding a person. In fact, it can be counterproductive to start analyzing every client who comes in the door. Rather it is helpful to simply be aware of these differences and consider their potential application to our work.

---

4. Howard Gardner, *Frames of Mind, 10th Edition,* Basic Books (1993).

The basic lesson here is that we cannot assume that other people think, react, feel, learn and understand the way we do. That assumption is the greatest barrier to understanding out clients.

People Learn Differently

Teachers learn to know their students and the different ways they learn. As discussed previously, to a great degree the relationship of a paralegal to her client is often one of instructing the client as a teacher does a student. Thus it is important for an effective paralegal to know her client's way of learning.

Our tendency is to sit with our clients and talk to them. For some clients, that works just fine. For others, talk simply does not sink in. I am reminded of a cartoon of a dog listening to its owner speak. It basically hears "blah, blah, blah, blah, WALK, blah, blah, blah, FIDO, blah, blah, DINNER." Sometimes it is like that for clients listening to attorneys and paralegals. Because they key on certain words (deed, will, settlement, witness) they can react appropriately, but they have not really understood what we have said.

Some people learn better when they see what they are supposed to learn. You will inform this client best by using diagrams, charts and other visual aids, a video of a deposition being conducted, for example. Others learn best by reading. Still others learn best by doing, for example by running through a fifteen minute practice deposition. You can best instruct your client if you develop the ability to either learn your client's learning style or develop the ability to present each important item in multiple ways to every client. The second is fairly certain, the first is more efficient.

People React Differently

People react differently to almost everything that can cause them to react. We can best serve our clients if we know something about how they react, especially how they react to stress and conflict. This may be most obvious in the context of litigation, but remember that almost everything with which we are not familiar causes stress, and almost every legal process from buying/selling a house, adopting a child, creating a business to facing criminal charges will be unfamiliar to our clients and therefore a source of stress. Since people seldom seek the services of an attorney, even going to the law office can create some stress. In addition, the reason they come to our office is usually stressful. Stress, in turn, can lead to many reactions—nervousness, disorientation, irritability, shyness and so on.

Recognizing that each client is likely to feel, to a greater or lesser extent, as a stranger in a strange land when it comes to legal processes, it is helpful for the paralegal and attorney to know something about how the clients react to that stress and take steps to relieve it. Often knowing the client's reaction to stress will allow us to determine the extent to which they will be able to fulfill their role on the legal team with or without assistance.

This is particularly true when it come to a client's approach to conflict. Many, if not most of what lawyers do involves conflict. Again, this is most obvious in the context of litigation, but it applies to many other legal processes. When our client is trying to buy a house, our client and the seller have a common purpose, but their interests often conflict on everything from the selling price to the scheduling of the closing.

We will deal with approaches to conflict again in the next chapter. But this area is important enough to our management of clients that we will also examine here the standard approaches and how they might affect your client. The basic approaches can be characterized in several ways. I prefer avoidance, accommodation, compromise, competition and collaboration. None of these approaches is "right" or "wrong." None may even be "best" or "worse." Each may have its place and time when it is the best approach to a particular conflict. Our goal at the moment is simply to recognize the approaches and be aware of the danger they pose to our management of our clients.

- *Avoidance.* Clients often want to deal with conflict by pretending it does not exist. Conflict can be unpleasant. This approach poses several problems in the legal context. A client who wants to block out the very fact of the conflict can find it difficult to attend to what must be done. They will put off answers to interrogatories and the like to the last minute or later if you let them. They want to do what you told them to do, but will consistently have excuses for not doing so. This can spin out quite destructively as the client begins to avoid your calls because you represent the conflict they are trying to deny. They become embarrassed and ashamed of what they may view as a weakness, but project their feelings onto you. They may even begin to resent you.

  This situation can easily get out of control, but you can manage this type of client if you recognize the signs when they first appear. First, do not reprimand the client for delays as this only reinforces their desire to avoid. Instead, express understanding the unpleasantness of their situation and their desire to wish it away. Ask whether they have any support network to help them through. Break what they have to do down into smaller pieces and praise them for accomplishing each piece. Familiar-ize them with the process to make it less frightening. Make more frequent *friendly* calls to them. Remind them they are not alone but are part of the legal team. Assure them through your professionalism that they will be protected from the brunt of the conflict itself, if not the results.

- *Accommodation.* Sometimes the client will acknowledge the conflict, but be motivated to make agreements they will later regret in order to avoid the conflict. Once the conflict is settled and they look back, they regret their decisions. Since they look at the attorney and paralegal as their protectors, they hold the results against the attorney and paralegal. In worse case scenarios, the client blames the attorney for what they now consider a bad result and file a malpractice claim.

    Again, this problem can best be avoided by recognizing its potential early on. If this is done, the attorney can take steps such as making sure the client is given time to "cool off" before signing any final agreement. She may also make greater efforts to conduct negotiations without the client having to meet face to face with the other side. At the very least, she can see that a solid record is made for purposes of rebutting any claims of improper representation the client makes later.

- *Compromise.* Compromise avoids some of the problems of the two approaches we have discussed so far. Together you acknowledge the conflict and find a resolution that may leave both parties feeling they got something, as opposed to accommodation in which one party simply satisfies the interests of the other. On the downside, it does mean giving up something also. Depending on the issue, a true compromise can be quite satisfying to the client, but there are issues where it does not work. Some issues are a matter of principle and not susceptible to compromise. If a client feels that way, then compromising may leave them feeling no better than accommodation in the end. At other times, compromise leaves both parties without anything of real value. It is appropriate when half a loaf is indeed better than none. But if each of the parties needs a ten-foot ladder, a compromise that leaves both with five feet of the ladder does neither of them good. In fact, since both parties are left unsatisfied, it doubles the downside of the accommodation approach; but at the moment we are focused only on our client.

- *Competition.* This client simply *must* win. Trying to persuade them to compromise will waste everyone's time and lead to resentment. Instead, the attorney will likely focus on pointing out to the client how a particular result *is a win* for the client. We see this frequently with political spokespersons who seem to be able to make even the worse loss a positive for their candidate. They might point out that their client lost 80%

to 20%, but it was a win because the polls said their candidate would only get 15%! This can work with competitive clients also, especially near the end of negotiations. Sometimes they can be assured they won simply because the last concession was made by the other side even if it is a small concession. You can be a tremendous help to your attorney by identifying this approach early and informing your attorney.

· *Collaboration.* This is also referred to as the "problem solving" approach. It is especially useful when those involved in a conflict will have to work together as you and your attorney will. However, it generally requires more time, attention and thought than the other approaches. Generally people approach conflict as if they always involved splitting that loaf of bread when quite frequently that is not the case. Remember that ten-foot ladder. Dividing it in two did neither party any good. Taking turns using it would allow both to climb to the top. Unfortunately, it takes two to do this tango and collaborative clients can become quite frustrated when the other side takes another approach. Also, collaboration requires that both parties be honest about their real concerns and open to hearing the real concerns of the other side. This may lead clients to reveal too much too soon for the attorney. Again, you can help the attorney manage the client by identifying this approach early.

As stated above, there is no right or wrong approach to conflict. Our client's approach is simply what it is. Knowing what that approach is gives us an advantage in managing the client and the client's expectations. It also allows us to avoid unnecessary stress and additional conflict that can arise when the client's approach differs from the attorney's.

People Have Different Needs

Needy People

In a general sense, some people are just more needy than others. They need feedback, reassurance, attention and overall hand-holding. Some express this in a demanding way; others in a pleading or whiny way. Still others complain. This type of client will not simply go away. (And if they pay their bills, we do not want them to go away.) They cannot just be ignored, the functional equivalent of the avoidance approach to conflict. Yet, because setting parameters with such clients can be the source of conflict, we are often tempted to do just that.

While needy clients cannot be avoided, they can be managed in a way that minimizes the annoyance they cause. Many can be managed simply by applying the techniques we have already discussed.

- Establish clear rules in the initial interview and stick to them. Explain when and how your office communicates with clients. We discussed possible methods of doing this in Chapter One, "Managing Your Time."
- Honor your communication rules. If the rule is all phone calls will be returned within twenty-four hours, follow that rule. The client is less likely to make repeated calls if they know you *will not* take or respond to them except according to your established policies, but you *will* follow those policies yourself.
- Establish telephone appointments. If you simply put off a client because you are busy, they will continually call back to see if you are still busy. Instead, specify a time to when they can call and reach you, then be available when they call.
- Give your client a tablet of paper specifically designated for them to note questions, concerns, and thoughts about their matter, and instruct them to call once a week with the tablet available. Politely and diplomatically make sure they know how to write.
- Keep the client informed.
  ◦ Send them copies of every letter you mail in their case.
  ◦ Send them copies of every document that comes in *with a standard description of what the document is and how it affects them.* This can be done with standardized information sheets developed by your office. Sometimes a simple cover sheet with simple notices like these will suffice: "This is being provided to you for your information and your file. You do not need to respond or take any action." "With this letter we requested a title examination of your property. Title examinations normally take at least ten days. Please mark that day on your calendar."
  ◦ Use email to keep them posted. As discussed previously, email must also be controlled, but it can be. At the very least, you can respond to it on your own terms, and there is a written record that you did respond. However, be careful with email. Because it is not a formal letter, we can become cavalier about it and are not always mindful of what we say. This is especially true when writing to the attorney *about* clients. Remember, any email you sent may someday be read by the Board of Bar Overseers or other attorney conduct disciplinary entity.
- Encourage the client to use whatever support resources they have available—family members, clergy, social workers and others—to support them with non-legal issues. Remind them, however, that they should not speak to anyone about the facts or strategy of their legal matter.

- Give the client homework. They are likely to feel less needy if they feel useful. Note, however, that some clients do not appreciate homework. Their attitude is that they are paying you to get things done and resent being told to do it themselves. Again, one size does not fit all, so there is a premium on knowing your client.

Remain professional in dealing with all clients, including the annoying ones. One way to influence behavior is to exemplify the desired behavior. Many clients will model their conduct after yours as they become more involved in the legal team. Once you bring them into the legal team and show them how professional, disciplined and competent the other members of the team are, the needy clients become reassured and less needy.

Hierarchy of Needs

In 1943 Abraham Maslow published a psychological theory about human needs.[5] It contained a depiction of human needs that is widely used in many fields, but especially in the educational field. Again, we need not become experts in his field to apply the basic concepts to our work. Basically he noted that there is a hierarchy to the importance of human needs. While not the depiction Maslow used, Figure 5.1 shows a similar hierarchy.

Our application of this theory need not be very sophisticated. We need only be aware that clients may perceive needs differently than we do, and those differences will affect their understanding and approaches to legal situations. The same is true of unstated needs.

I once had a case that I was certain would bring two to three times as much from a jury as the defendant was offering to pay to settle the case. Naturally my recommendation to the client was that he reject the offer. He, however, was anxious to accept it despite my insistence that acceptance was not in his best interest. After pressing the point a bit, the client told me his house was under foreclosure, something he found embarrassing and had not wanted to admit. His reasoning was that it was better to have less now and save his home, than to have more later but force his family into homelessness in the meantime.

This client's need for security and protection for him and his family was more important than his need for just compensation for his injury. Of course, if he did become homeless, his ability to assist in the prosecution of his case would have been greatly diminished and lessened the likely verdict from a jury.

---

5. A.H. Maslow, A Theory of Human Motivation, Psychological Review 50(4) (1943): 370–96.

Figure 5.4

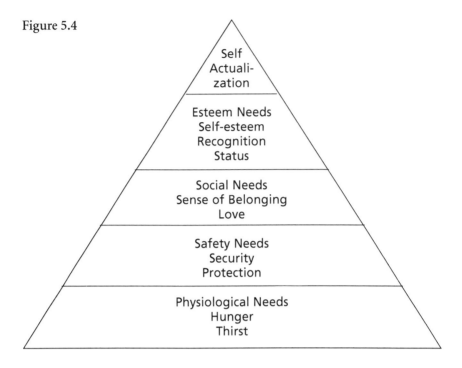

Knowing this, our attention shifted to negotiations with the foreclosing bank. Once we worked out a deal with the bank to keep the client in his house until the case resolved, the client was able to re-focus and agreed to take the case to trial. Confronted with a newly resolute and determined plaintiff, the defendant shortly raised his offer and the case settled on fair terms.

The lesson is that we must at least know enough about our client to understand and assist them with non-legal needs that interfere with the processing of their legal matter. We cannot expect them to be effective, cooperative members of the legal team if their more basic needs are not being met.

D. Working Together for a Manageable Client

Let's take another look at NaShana's client, Joan, and see how NaShana might have managed Joan better by applying what we have learned in this chapter.

First, the client, Joan, did not show up on time, which was inexcusable since NaShana had sent her a letter stating the date, time and location of the mediation. When Joan did show up she appeared disheveled, dirty, groggy, disoriented and irritable.

Joan works as a maid in a hospital across town. The maids rotate shifts on a two week basis. This week is the first of her two weeks working the shift that runs from 11:00 p.m. to 8:00 a.m. Once she clocked out, she quickly changed from her maid outfit into her street clothes, but did not have time to shower or clean up before rushing to the bus for the cross-town trip to the mediator's office. She missed the initial bus and had to wait thirty minutes for the next one that would take her where she needed to be.

NaShana had performed the normal procedure of scheduling the mediation and informing the client by letter. If instead she had called Joan first, she could have avoided these problems by scheduling the mediation in the afternoon.

> *Even when alone with NaShana and her attorney, the client seemed confrontational. It was almost as if she did not understand that NaShana and the attorney were on her side.*

In addition to being exhausted from being up all night, Joan does not like conflict. The stress it puts her into "fight or flight" mode. Her impression of how disputes get resolved in the legal system comes from TV and movies where the client sits silently at the side of the attorney in a courtroom where there is no direct contact between the parties. Since no on told her anything different, she assumed that was what would happen today. Since her attorney did not consistently stand up for her and "fight" for her, she switched into her own fight mode, directing some of her frustration and fight towards the people she thought were going to fight for her.

> *She certainly didn't understand the role of the mediator who she kept on demanding "rule in her favor." She got very upset every time the mediator said anything that questioned her position or suggested that she should consider weaknesses in her case. More than once, she implied that the mediator must be "in the other side's pocket."*

Again, Joan is confronted with a reality that does not meet her expectations. NaShana and her attorney had told Joan at the first meeting that her case would go to mediation and that there would be a person there called a mediator who would help resolve the case, but she had no conception or an erroneous conception of what mediation was or how a mediator was supposed to act. To the extent any of this was explained in the letter NaShana had sent her, it was just legal mumble-jumble to Joan. Since her expectations were not met, she assumed the worse, especially as her lack of sleep and the stress of the situation wore on her.

> *Joan's irritation grew every time the mediator met privately with the other side, especially when the meetings went for more than a few min-*

utes. She was very impatient and kept looking at the clock. Well before the
mediation was done, Joan insisted she could not stay longer and walked
out, leaving NaShana's attorney to explain her sudden absence.

Joan had not understood how long mediation takes. She probably would have had the same problem with a court hearing unless she was informed of the likely time requirements. After all, trials start and finish in an hour on TV, two hours maximum if it's a movie. She had not made child care arrangements and her daughter was arriving home from morning kindergarten. The need to provide safety and security to her daughter overcame her legal needs. She could have explained that before leaving, but at that point she was exhausted, frustrated and angry.

Knowing her client and communicating with her client would have made all the difference in NaShana's mediation experience with Joan. It takes more time, more work and more thought, but the pay off for that effort is tremendous. Also, there are ways to minimize the effort required. For example, you can develop checklists to go through with the clients that cover non-legal needs that might interfere with a legal event such as transportation, child-care and work schedules. A short conversation with the client will allow the client to begin making arrangements in advance and for you to work around obstacles. As noted above, videos explaining and showing examples of depositions, mediations and even real estate closings can be purchased or developed. Clients can watch such videos in a conference room so the other members of the legal team can be available but attend to other matters at the same time.

E. Ethical and Malpractice Considerations

You are likely well versed in the two biggest ethical obligations that arise in dealing with clients—confidentiality and the unauthorized practice of law, so I will not cover them here. There are three ethical and malpractice considerations I would like to bring to your attention though, each of which are based on our discussion in this chapter.

- We discussed your need to be professional, non-judgmental and objective especially by not allowing dislike of the client or what the client has done or proposes to do affect the way you do your job. Frankly, sometimes this is just not possible. Even recognizing everyone's right to be represented in a criminal trial, some attorneys have cases they simply will not take, because it would be a violation of their obligation to take them if their objectivity is so affected that they cannot fully and effectively represent the client. You may also find yourself in that position. If so, make your attorney aware of it as soon as possible.

- Many client complaints of malpractice and unethical behavior are based on misunderstanding or simple lack of knowledge on the part of client. When they lose a case, they feel it is because their attorney did nothing. They feel that way because they have no knowledge to the contrary. Their phone calls were not returned, they received no copies of correspondence and court documents, they were not informed of what to expect and so on. Attorneys successfully defend against such complaints, but waste many dollars and hours in doing so. That waste is often unnecessary. The principles and techniques we've discussed in this chapter are not just good for the legal process. They can avoid many such complaints.

- If an attorney practices long enough it is almost inevitable that she will face ethical and malpractice complaints, many of which will be unjustified. It is important that there be adequate and comprehensive records to document the client file. A client may allege that he called twenty times in two weeks with no response. A telephone call log shows he called three times, each of which received a response within twenty-four hours, even if the responsive phone calls resulted only in repeated busy signals. This not only deflates that claim but casts doubt on any other complaint he makes.

  Written memos to the file are also important. Even though such memos, like emails, are informal, each such memo must be written with an eye towards the possibility that it could be read by a judge or jury in a malpractice case or by the Bar Counsel. Be especially careful what you say about your client. Convey the fact that your client is a confrontational, uncooperative, stubborn and drunk moron, but be careful and diplomatic about how you do it.

Conclusion

The effective, empowered paralegal manages clients well. The client is part of the legal team, which means more than simply that without him there is no need for either the paralegal or attorney and no money to fund the law office. However, the client is the member of the team who knows least about the law and her role in the team. It is essential that the paralegal and the attorney keep the client informed about what is being done for her and why, and what she needs to do for the outcome to be successful.

The keys to managing your client are the same keys you use to manage your time, workload, docket and files—preparation, understanding, communication, clarity and organization. Recognize the role of the client on the legal team and prepare the client for that role. Use your knowledge of the differences in people, especially those that present barriers to understanding—cultural, linguistic and learning differences—to ensure that your client understands the legal process, what she can expect from you and the attorney and what you expect from her.

Now that you have the tools you need to manage the client, we can move to Chapter Six where we will take on a more difficult task—managing your attorney.

Chapter Six

Managing Your Attorney — Don't Bother Me, Just Do It!

The title to this chapter is not meant to be taken literally. It is not your job to manage your attorney. And no matter how tempting it might be, it is not a job you should take upon yourself. However, the effective, empowered paralegal manages well the paralegal's relationship with the attorney within the legal team. Both the paralegal and attorney must know, and respect, their roles and those of the other; their abilities and those of the other. It is essential that the paralegal understand what the attorney expects of him and the attorney understand what the paralegal can and cannot do for her. We want to avoid becoming like Henry:

> Once again Henry is sitting at his desk virtually seething with irritation and frustration. It's been one of THOSE days and his attorney seems to be blaming everything on him. When he arrived at this desk he found a research memo he had done for his attorney, Michael, the day before. Attached to the memo was a post-it telling Henry to call a restaurant to make a reservation for Michael and his wife for dinner that evening.
> But what riled Henry was the red ink scrawled over the memo. Michael was not happy with it and it appeared that much of what Henry had done had missed the point of the assignment. When Henry met with Michael, Michael reprimanded him. Henry apologized but felt the reprimand was unfair. Michael is the attorney. He should have been more clear about what he wanted, about the issues that concerned him and about the format in which he expected the results to be presented. After all, it is Michael's job to supervise Henry. To top it off, as Henry had scurried out of Michael's office and back to his desk, Michael had made a rude comment about Henry's tie — a bolo type like the one made by Navajo Indians that he had seen Hank Williams, Jr. wearing (and looked great with the Toby Keith cowboy boots he was wearing).
> Henry felt Michael had no respect for him, and he was quickly losing what respect he had for Michael. Henry was well trained and competent.

He could do far more for Michael than Michael was allowing him to do and could do his assignments better if Michael was just clear about what was expected. Instead, his time is filled with very un-paralegal type tasks like making dinner reservations, and Michael finds fault with everything he does. All Henry thinks he can do is sit and take it—and seethe. While Henry is well educated and competent as a paralegal, he's wrong about this.

Certainly to be members of an effective legal team, Michael and Henry have to respect each other as professionals. This can be difficult at times because of uncertainty on the part of both the paralegal and the attorney as to what the role of each of them is on the legal team. So we'll start this chapter by taking a short look at that topic. Then we'll examine what it means for a paralegal to be a professional from the perspective of an attorney and how to prevent some of the problems that can occur in the paralegal/attorney relationship through communication.

A. The Attorney and Paralegal as Part of the Legal Team

Understanding Your Attorney's Understanding of "Paralegal"

It is not surprising that there is so much confusion over the role of paralegals and their relationship to the attorneys on legal teams. The extent of the confusion varies significantly depending on a number of factors, including the size of the law firm and the length of time attorneys in the firm have been using paralegals. Large law firms in larger cities tend to have been employing paralegals for a long time and have worked out must of the "kinks." They will generally *inform* a new hired paralegal of exactly what their role is to be in the firm. (Some small firms have also progressed to this point.) This does not, however, necessarily solve the problems that arise in the various attorney/paralegal teams within those firms.

Smaller firms and many attorneys may have very little experience with paralegals. While they have been convinced they need a paralegal (and they *do*), they may not have a very clear idea of what a paralegal really is. After all, paralegals as a distinct member of the legal team are a relatively new phenomenon. In fact, it was only relatively recently that the American Bar Association and the National Association of Legal Assistants agreed upon a definition:

> A person qualified by education, training, and/or work experience, who is employed or retained by a lawyer, law office, corporation, gov-

ernment agency or other entity who performs specifically delegated substantive legal work, for which a lawyer is responsible.

As is so often the case in law, however, having a definition helps define the word, but does not necessarily help understand what and who a paralegal is.

Do not assume that your attorney really understands what a paralegal is. Here are just some of the reasons they may not understand:

- Some attorneys do not understand the distinction between a legal secretary and a paralegal. In some small firms, especially a single attorney office, all the staff is used to doing about everything. There is no file clerk, so everyone just does the filing when they are using a file. While there are differences in the positions of the staff, there are no clear job descriptions. This blurring of lines in daily practice can cause confusion.
- Often the problem goes deeper than that. There is substantial confusion in the legal system itself. The ABA and NALA may have agreed upon a common definition. You know this from school, but few attorneys know the definition much less understand it. In fact, while many attorneys, paralegals and legal assistants feel there is no difference between a paralegal and a legal assistant, others draw a rather unclear distinction. For them there is an hierarchy that runs some thing like this: receptionist, secretary, legal secretary, legal assistant, paralegal. Almost nobody has a clear idea of exactly where the lines are drawn between the various stages in the hierarchy. In areas where this distinction is made, generally the paralegal is more educated and/or more experienced than the legal assistant and is often paid more. Similarly, the paralegal is given more responsibility for substantive legal work while the legal assistant may have more clerical and/or secretarial duties.
- Your attorney may think that paralegals are more than a legal secretary and less than an associate attorney, but be quite vague as to where they fall between those two goal posts. As a result, the attorney may expect you to do work that is really attorney work and give you less guidance and supervision that you need and deserve. Or she may be unaware of just how much help you can be and give you tasks you feel underutilize your talent because she views you as a "fancy" legal secretary or "just" a legal assistant.
- The ABA/NALA definition does not help such attorneys much. Unlike the attorney who must meet specific educational and licensing requirements, how a paralegal becomes a paralegal is a bit of a mystery to many both in and outside the profession. There was a time when a person could become an attorney just through experience by "apprenticing" to an established lawyer, or by studying and passing the bar exam, but those days

are long gone. So it can be unclear to an attorney (and almost everyone else) just what qualifies a paralegal to be a paralegal.

- The definition says "education, training, and/or work experience," but how much of each is needed? Not long ago, there were no formal paralegal education programs. Most paralegals simply moved up the receptionist, secretary, legal secretary and legal assistant ladder by gaining more and more responsibility as a result of more and more experience, which gave the attorney more and more confidence in their ability to handle that responsibility. At what point did they become paralegals— after five years? Ten? Fifteen? At what point did the responsibility level become that of a paralegal rather than that of a legal assistant? What is "substantive legal work?"
- The present status of paralegal education is no less confusing to many attorneys. What is the difference, in terms of the work the paralegal can perform, between a paralegal certificate, an associates degree in paralegal studies and a bachelors degree in paralegal studies? What does it mean to be certified? Is being certified the same as having a certificate? Who does the certification?

When I am asked to give advice to attorneys on training their paralegals, I often discover that it is the attorneys that need to be trained on the utilization of their paralegals! They are perfectly competent, sometimes extremely competent, attorneys, but know little about the capabilities of their own staff.

Short of having me there to advise your attorney, you must communicate your abilities and the limits of your abilities to your attorney. You must let him know what you can do and what you can not, when and how much guidance you need, and the like. We will discuss the communication itself, but first we need to establish the basic premise: you, like the attorney, are a professional. How do we do that? We show it by *being* professional.

B. The Paralegal as a Professional

A Professional Is Ethical

Here I'm not talking about the legal ethics you studied in class, although for attorneys the rules governing their conduct are often referred to as "Rules of Professional Conduct." Certainly every attorney will want you to know, respect and apply the rules of legal ethics demanded of them by the court or other body that supervises and disciplines them as professionals. They will require you to do so even if they are not naturally inclined towards following them simply to avoid discipline. Most attorneys are aware that they are responsible for what their staff does even if they do not understand the particular role of a paralegal and their special obligation to supervise paralegals.

What you need to show your attorney is not only that you understand the ethical requirements of the legal profession, but that you have and follow a personal ethic that raises you to the level of a professional. Now, I am not suggesting that non-professionals are not ethical or never have to make ethical choices. My remarks are made in the context of our discussion of you as a paralegal having or wanting more responsibility—responsibility reserved to professionals as a result of their specialized knowledge and experience. With that responsibility comes more opportunity for non-ethical choices and a higher expectation for ethical behavior.

Basically we are talking about the elements of character: integrity, reliability, self-discipline, courtesy, respect for others and even lesser attributes such as punctuality. Everyone has their own list. Boy Scouts follow a "law" that requires them to be trustworthy, loyal, helpful, friendly, courteous, kind, obedient, cheerful, thrifty, brave, clean and reverent. This list works for Boy Scouts, and properly interpreted and applied it can work for professionals also. The list itself is not as important as the attributes each list incorporates.

But enough of the moralizing, what does this mean in the law office? It means being aware of your own conduct and the fact that your status is determined not just by the quantity of your work, but by the quality of your work and how you behave while perform that work. It would be nice to be able to sum it all up by saying you should have a good "work ethic" or that you should "work hard and do a good job." But it is really more than that. For example, you will not be viewed as professional and worthy of professional responsibilities if you:

- Are not reliable.
  - Be where you are supposed to be when you are supposed to be there. While everyone runs into traffic jams, flat tires and the like, reliable persons are not habitually late or absent. Many instances of tardiness or absence could be avoided by proper planning of the sort discussed in Chapter Two. Do not leave the office early just because your attorney is in court and no one will notice or run personal errands on your way to deliver a brief, deed or contract across town unless you have discussed it in advance.
  - Complete your work on time. The excuses you used in school will carry little weight with your attorney, less with a client and none at all with a court. Plan your work so it will be done on time *even if something goes wrong.*

- ◦ Avoid making promises you can not keep. Be honest about what you can and cannot do and how long it will take to do it. We will discuss dealing with unrealistic expectations on the part of the attorney later. For now, avoid creating those expectations on the part of co-workers, attorneys and clients.
- • Are not honest.

  This can be a tough one. Sometimes you will be asked to be just a bit not-so-honest such as when you are asked to tell a client the attorney has just left for the courthouse when she is still in the office. The rightness and wrongness of such "white lies" is a matter that cannot be treated fully here. Personally I believe that the best policy is to be as honest as possible with the people with whom both the lawyer and the paralegal deal whether it be clients, co-workers, court personnel, etc. Regardless of how situations like this are resolved, you should strive for an honest relationship with your attorney. This does not mean you have to be the one to point out he has put on twenty pounds and needs to exercise more. But be honest about yourself.

  - ◦ Avoid dishonesty when you have made a mistake. Don't try to cover it up. No one is perfect. Honesty can initiate steps to help you avoid making the same mistake again.
  - ◦ Avoid dishonesty in explaining why you are late for work, taking time off and the like.
  - ◦ Avoid dishonesty when stating what you can and cannot do. Be frank about your own limitations both in terms of time and competence. Ask for assistance and training.
- • Are not trustworthy.
  - ◦ During the course of working as a legal team you will learn personal information about other members of the team, sometimes through disclosure, sometimes through happenstance. Avoid any discussion of such information inside or outside the legal team unless you have express and clear permission. In fact, it is best to avoid all forms of gossip. Certainly nothing that occurs in the office—including office politics—should be discussed with anyone outside of the office.
  - ◦ You are expected to work independently. While the attorney is responsible for supervising you, she sends you off with a task and expects it to be done competently and efficiently. Avoid using your time at work for personal errands, Internet browsing or shopping, and personal phone calls.
- • Do only what you are told to do.
  - ◦ I'm not suggesting that you *don't* do what you are told to do by your attorney, but if that is all you do—put in your time, do what you are

told and wait for the next task to be assigned, you will not be considered professional.

- ◦ Take the initiative. Suggest ways you could be helpful. When your assigned work is done, don't just pass the time — let the attorney know you are ready for the next assignment. Just *being there* is not enough. Make yourself useful.
- ◦ If you truly have "down time," learn something. Find out how to do something you do not already know how to do that will be useful to you in your capacity as a member of the legal team.
- ◦ Offer to help others who are busy. Avoid distracting other staff by talking about topics unrelated to whatever they are working on.
- ◦ Be positive and enthusiastic. Do your work with a high level of energy and dedication. Help your office maintain a positive and pleasant working environment.
- • Do not get along with others.
  - ◦ You are part of a team. If you are reading this you are clearly a valuable member of that team. But the team will only function if you work together as a team, rather as a group of individuals joined together for a purpose.
  - ◦ Cooperate and collaborate. Understand what others do and what your role is on the team. You are making a good start at this by reading this and the chapter on clients.

It is not possible to cover every aspect of this topic here. The short answer is that in order to be considered a professional you have to develop and demonstrate a *professional work ethic.*

While people do enter the legal profession to make money, I believe few enter it *only* to make money. The legal profession, and what we do, has a purpose that goes well beyond simply making money. It is not just a job. It has value that goes beyond the dollars produced during the year. Value what you do, because *you* do it. Resolve to do it as well as you can. Be aware of the purpose of belonging to the legal profession and be part of that purpose. The professional work ethic will fall in place.

There are, however, a few more things to consider. They are the topic of the next section.

A Professional Is … Professional

To a degree, professionalism is like art — we cannot define it, but we know it when we see it. If you've read and understood the first few chapters of this book you are well on your way to being a professional. You know how to manage your time, workload, calendar and clients. You are efficient and capable. You give your office not only the time but the effort for which you are paid. You have a good positive attitude and will do what it takes within reasonable practical, ethical and legal limits. There are just a few things we need to add. Some of them are:

- Have and use the skills necessary for your position
  - Computer skills
  - Writing skills
    | You should have or develop the ability to write clearly, concisely and in a well-organized fashion.
    | Know and use the rules of grammar, spelling and punctuation. Use, but do not rely on, computer software spelling- and grammar-checking tools.
    | Proofread your work. Have other people proofread your work. Draft and re-draft.
  - Reading skills
    | Read carefully. Analyze what you read and be sure you understand it, especially instructions or requests from your attorney.
    | Read for comprehension rather than memorization.
    | Read for examples of good writing.
  - Communication skills
    | Speak professionally. Avoid slang. Think before you speak.
    | Speak clearly. Avoid mumbling, slurring of words and the like.
    | Pronounce words correctly.
  - Listening skills
    | Look at the people to whom your are speaking and who are speaking to you.
    | Ask questions to clarify anything that seems unclear to you.
    | Ask yourself whether what you heard could be interpreted more than one way and then take measures to ensure you have interpreted it correctly.
    | Pay attention to body language.
    | Avoid interrupting other speakers.
- Become involved in professional associations
  - Be active in a local branch of the National Association of Legal Assistants, National Federation of Paralegal Association, or similar groups.
  - Subscribe to paralegal listservs and participate in discussions.
  - Read, learn from and contribute to publications designed for paralegal.
  - Become certified by your organization.

- Attend seminars and conference, especially those that include continuing legal education credit.
- Maintain a professional appearance

  The legal profession, unlike the medical profession, is not characterized by a particular uniform, but certain modes of dress are considered appropriate for the professional and others are not. A professional image is important not only for others, but also for yourself. The way you look sends a message to clients, attorneys and you. Any sort of uniform helps you make the transition from normal life to work life. A business suit or comparable dress enhances your own perception of yourself as a professional.

  The general rule is that you want to be noticed for the high quality of the work you do and for what you add to the legal team, not for what you wear. Keep the following in mind:
  - A professional appearance is neither "hot" nor "cool." You may be fortunate enough to meet your soul-mate or your next date at work, but avoid dressing as though you are looking for them.
  - Professional dress is not short, tight, clinging or revealing.
  - Professional dress looks good, not sexy (although looking good can be sexy if you have the right attitude).
  - Professional dress, except for shoes, belt and coats, is not leather.
  - Professional dress is not flashy.
  - Dress appropriately for the circumstances. Office wear and court wear may or may not be the same depending on your office. Take the time to find out. Take cues from how your attorney and other professionals in the office dress. If you are in Montana, cowboy boots may be fine; probably not in Baltimore.
  - Wash and iron your clothes. Shine your shoes.
  - Coordinate your clothing, jewelry and shoes.
  - You are part of the legal team and part of gaining the client's business, trust and confidence. You are not likely to do that if you dress inappropriately or look like a slob.
  - When in doubt, ask.

Professional appearance goes beyond dress
  - Be clean and neat. Wash and comb your hair, trim and clean your nails, shower and bathe regularly and often. (Once a week is not "often.") Brush your teeth.
  - Cover tattoos and remove non-standard body-piercing. Earrings are fine for women, but seldom acceptable for men. Customs may change, but more than that is not considered professional as of 2009.
  - Avoid "exotic" hairstyles and excessive or gaudy jewelry.

- Go easy on make-up, perfume, cologne or other scents. Less is often best.
- Rightly or wrongly, overweight and obese persons are often regarded as less professional.

Professional appearance includes your attitude. Remember other people read body language also. What are you saying? Are you projecting an image of confidence, organization, reliability, good judgment and competence?

- Avoid scowling, frowning and the like when it is not called for or intended.
- Sit up straight.
- Avoid slouching.
- Look at people when you talk to them or they talk to you.
- Avoid folding your arms and looking down during discussions. It gives the appearance you are not open to discussion.

- Maintain professional etiquette

  You do not need to memorize a bunch of rules like which fork you use to eat your salad, but etiquette is important in any business environment. For the most part, you will do fine if you remember what you were taught in kindergarten.

  - Be considerate of others.
  - Avoid interrupting others when they are speaking
  - Be respectful.
  - Apologize when you make a mistake.
  - Realize that you do make mistakes.
  - Arrive on time or early.
  - Avoid taking calls and using your cell phone during conversations.
  - Speak firmly, but not loudly. Moderate your tone.
  - Develop a system for remembering dates (birthdays, etc.) and other items of importance (her son is due to graduate this year) about those with whom you deal regularly.
  - Avoid gossiping. Speak well of others.
  - Be aware of cultural differences.
  - Return phone calls.
  - Use proper spelling, grammar and punctuation in emails.
  - DO NOT USE ALL CAPS IN EMAILS.

The Good News

By now you may be wondering whether being a professional is such a good idea. I often feel as though I should apologize for making professionalism sound boring. The good news is that it when you focus on it the way we have done here, it sounds a lot worse than it is. In fact being professional, acting professional and knowing you are professional is quite rewarding and more than makes up for any down side. You still get to wear the leather mini-skirt and hula-girl ties—just not at work. At work, you get the immense satisfaction of being regarded as, and being given the responsibility of, a professional.

C. Understanding the Attorney

Your attorney is another member of the legal team, but he is not *just* another member. The attorney is quite definitely the leader, director and manager of the team. More important, she is *the attorney*. And she is your employer (or at least higher up on the employment ladder in the firm that employs you.) All this means you must get along with her whether you like her or not. Sometimes attorneys are not as professional as you are. They can be arrogant, pompous and rude. They can be wrong and refuse to admit it. They can be less professional than you and see no inconsistency in expecting you to be professional. In the end you have to have respect for their role as an attorney in your legal team whether you respect them as individuals or even as attorneys. (The same applies to other paralegals on your team or in your office.)

Attorneys are people with as many faults as everyone else and can be just as difficult, sometimes more difficult, to understand than anyone else. They are individuals, so no one set of rules can tell you how to deal with each and every attorney. However, it is helpful to gain as much understanding of your attorney as possible. We started this in the first part of this chapter when we discussed understanding the attorney's understanding of your role as a paralegal.

First some generalities you should keep in mind:

- Attorneys generally entered the profession of law because of the law and not because of the money. Sure they were aware lawyers can make a lot of money (and all too unaware of how many do not or what must be sacrificed to make that money), but they could have made money a lot of ways. They chose law for a reason. They are often either idealistic or formerly idealistic. The practice of law puts them in constant conflict between the ideal of "being a lawyer" and the practicalities of practicing law.
- Attorneys are generally fairly intelligent. You are highly unlikely to "put one past them," so it is best to be honest as a practical matter if not an ethical one. They made it through law school and passed the bar exam.

Further, they know they are intelligent, and therefore often feel, and act, superior. If you want to be successful as a paralegal you have to accept this fact. Often you must leave your ego at the door, because the attorney will not. If the two egos clash, his will win. It is a whole lot bigger.

- Attorneys are generally under a lot of pressure. Much of the pressure is to make money. They have to take on enormous caseloads to make enough money to pay the overhead (including your salary). Each of the cases in the caseload comes with deadlines, client expectations and the like. The good side of this coin is that you can be a hero by helping to relieve the pressure, meet the deadlines and make the money.
- Attorneys often become cynical. So many people, even their clients, lie to them that they often think they can believe no one. As we discuss in Chapter Seven, attorneys tend to think in terms of evidence and proof rather than facts. While this is essential to litigation, it can make life difficult.
- Attorneys are often conflicted by the knowledge that they must delegate and their innate desire to control.
- In many cases, the desire to control is not conjoined with a desire to be organized. If it is, they will object, but perhaps not vocally, to your efforts to re-organize their organization even if your way is better. If it is not, they will depend on you heavily for organization.
- Although they laugh politely at them, attorneys are tired of lawyer jokes. Generally, attorneys have a lot more integrity than public perception credits. Unfortunately this factor is general, not universal, and the exceptions get a lot of publicity.
- Even great attorneys are not necessarily good businesspersons or managers.

I am sure every attorney will have several more such generalities to add to the list if they had the time to think about it.

Knowing Your Attorney

One paralegal I knew felt she could figure her attorney out by reading his horoscope. It may have worked for her, but there are better ways. Everyone has their own style of doing things. It can be helpful for you to be aware of your attorney's style and your own style. Be aware of where they are compatible and where they are not. Emphasize the compatible and minimize the incompatible. Be aware of when she is acting the way she acts because it is her nature or style, and not as a personal matter with you. Given her position on the legal team, you should be particularly aware of her management style and approach to conflict. I can not tell you your particular attorney's style in any of these areas, but if we explore the various types in each area, you will be in a better position to work with her on the legal team.

Management Styles

Just about every expert that there is has their own way of categorizing and naming management styles. I am not an expert in management or management styles, so instead of relying on the "formal" categorization of any of the expert, in this discussion I will focus on the types of management I have seen used by attorneys during my career in terms of how they affect the legal team and your role on that team. Roughly, these styles are outgrowths or extensions of each attorney's personality. We will start with a look at two extremes.

The Non-manager Manager

Many attorneys are simply not managers. Their focus is, and has been, on law. They had no management training in college or law school, and may be in their first position requiring management skills. They are unprepared for, and may even subconsciously resent, the fact that they must both be a good attorney and a manager. Management tasks are viewed as a distraction from their real job of practicing law.

This is good for you if you yearn for independence and responsibility, but can go too far. A "don't bother me, just do it" attitude can even violate the attorney's ethical duty to provide you with adequate supervision. Short of that, it can put you in the position of "guessing" what needs to be done, in what order (i.e., prioritization) and how it is to be done. If you guess wrong, the attorney may blame it on you, but the fault is his. One solution to this problem is communication, a topic we take up in the next section.

The Micro-manager

This is the opposite of the non-manager. This attorney has not yet recognized your capabilities, or she may not herself have the capability of delegating tasks. She may feel it is necessary to look over your shoulder and manage the smallest details. This way of managing solves the problem of too little supervision and instruction, but is very difficult for the person being managed. There is no independence and very little responsibility other than following instructions to the letter. Unfortunately, this may be frustrating and often impossible to accomplish. The micro-manager is often difficult to please and likely to find some detail that is simply not done to her satisfaction. Communication is also important with this manager, but more in the sense of you improving your ability to listen and understand what is being communicated than in the sense of true two-way communication.

Between the Extremes

Fortunately most attorneys manage from somewhere in between these two extremes. The best adjust management style for different situations and different employees. However, even if they do not adjust, *you can.* Be aware of your attorney's style and adjust your approach to accommodate it. While you are a legal team and ideally I would like to see a team approach based on mutual respect and mutual understanding of each members role and capabilities, we do not live—or work—in a perfect world.

If the members of the team are unable to meld their styles, conflict inevitably arises. However, you can minimize the conflict and maximize opportunities for resolution by taking a step back, being aware of your attorney's management style and your reaction to it, and developing a plan based on communication, professionalism and respect, rather than feeling you have been personally slighted, or resorting to manipulation, avoidance and passive-aggressive behavior.

D. Approaches to Attorney/Paralegal Conflict and Collaboration

Any relationship depends on collaboration. Yet on occasion conflict arises in any relationship. Here I am not speaking of full-blown disputes or battles, but of simple conflicting interests, personalities, styles or even habits. For example, your desire for more responsibility may conflict with your attorney's habit of control, or your desire for more instruction and supervision may conflict with your attorney's desire not to focus, or inability to focus, on such tasks.

Conflict of this nature is somewhat inevitable. Conflict need not be bad, but it can yield bad results, especially if the conflict is not acknowledged and resolved. Simply letting it simmer benefits no one. So next we will review the styles or approaches to conflict. Being aware of these approaches will be beneficial not only in terms of your relationship with your attorney, but in all relationships. As we discussed in Chapter Five, knowing your client's approach to conflict is also helpful in managing the client.

Conflict arises between attorneys and their paralegals when they have wants, needs, desires or interests that are not only different, but that also appear that only one set of those wants can be achieved in any given situation. For these purposes, I assume that both the attorney and paralegal are acting professionally; for example, that you are doing your best to earn your salary as opposed to doing the least you can possibly do to earn your salary, and the attorney is doing his best to utilize your professional skills even if he lacks an understanding of what those skills truly are. Even when you both act professionally, conflicts can arise between your desire for the independence and responsibility of your profession and the attorney's desire for control; between your desire for supervision, guidance and clear instructions, and his desire that you just get the work done without bothering him. Such conflict is more apparent than real since both of you really want the same thing. You both benefit if you work as a team maximizing the contributions you each bring to that team.

In some situations one party may be, at least initially, unaware that the conflict exists. It is important that there be open communication between the attorney and paralegal not only to resolve conflict but also to create awareness that the conflict exists. With a demanding, authoritative, perhaps bullying attorney, you will be well aware of his desires and needs. A way must be found to inform him that you of yours without triggering a crisis. On the flip side, you must make it clear to the more reticent attorney that you are open to being made aware of potential conflicts between his expectations and your performance.

This awareness can sometimes be difficult to achieve because of the approach to conflict used either by the attorney, the paralegal or both. Generally, people will favor one of five approaches to conflict: avoidance, accommodation, competition, compromise or collaboration. Of course, no one is so fully committed to one approach that they can be strictly compartmentalized. Often people will use a blend of approaches, or they may use one approach at home and another at work, and so on.

There are many very good books in print on conflict resolution and the basic approaches to conflicts. We cannot go into great depth on each of them here, but let us take a brief look at the different approaches and how they might affect the attorney / paralegal relationship. Identifying your own gut-reaction approach with an awareness of that approach's benefits and pitfalls, will allow you to try new approaches when appropriate. Identifying the attorney's basic approach will allow you to react in a way most likely to minimize conflict and maximize conflict resolution.

- *Avoidance.* While conflicts arise whenever interest compete, that is, whenever there is the perception that one person's interests can only be satisfied when another person's interest is restricted, not all conflicts need to be raised to a level of a dispute or fight. Some battles are just not worth fighting and certainly there are many times when disagreements are simply not deserving of a battle. So, many times the best solution is to simply place the correct—minimal—value on the issue and move on. You like to use and were trained to use eleven-point fonts, but she demands twelve-point. To you, twelve-point seems all wrong. I understand, but here it may be best to simply move on.

Other times, avoidance is a mistake. If an issue is important, avoiding the conflict can lead to resentment, frustration, anger, manipulation and passive-aggressive conduct that only increase as the conflict simmers. Many such conflicts can be resolved if only the persons involved communicate about them. They cannot be resolved if the one harboring the resentment does not let the other person know the conflict exists! Simply doing it your way or manipulating an outcome breeds resentment on the other side. Ultimately, either you quit or are fired.

So, certainly you want to find a way to communicate your needs and the importance of the issue to the attorney in a diplomatic, non-confrontational way that acknowledges your needs, the attorney's needs and the fact that while you are both members of the legal team, she is your boss.

Just as important is that you communicate that you are professional enough for even the most reticent of attorneys to feel they can approach you when the need arises to discuss an issue important to them.

- *Accommodation.* Sometimes the realization that the battle is not worth fighting comes only after you or the attorney has conveyed to the other the fact there is a conflict. That's OK. Identifying and communicating a conflict does not mean you have to battle it out. If you have communicated your concerns and the attorney is simply unwilling to adjust, it may be best to accommodate—to give in. As long as you do so professionally, you may still come out with benefits, for example, the feeling on the part of an attorney that he "owes you one," or the acknowledgment that you are a team player worthy of trust. You can gain a lot of goodwill this way. Be mindful, however, that this approach can have long-range negative effects if you walk away feeling that you have lost, given in, been taken advantage of or need to keep score. Remember that I am suggesting that it is sometimes good for you *to choose* this approach. If you make a rational decision that this is the best approach for whatever reasons, then no one has taken advantage of you—you have made the choice.

  Also keep in mind, however, that your attorney may not be as enlightened as you are. When they accommodate you, they may feel that you owe them, that they have been taken advantage of and so on. Acknowledge what they have done for you. Be appreciative, not gloating. A little praise will go a long ways to minimizing negative after affects of this kind of conflict resolution.

- *Compromise.* Sometimes it seems that we as a people have lost the ability to compromise. Despite perennial talk of bipartisanship among politicians, many times it appears that all action is in a stalemate because each side refuses to compromise. Whether it is the "culture wars," religious or economic issues, many hold "principle" so dear that they would rather get nothing at all than to get half a loaf if it means the other side also gets half.

As a practical matter, business people and professionals simply cannot operate that way. In fact, compromise is part of almost any relationships whether it be parent/child, siblings, partnerships, employer/employee, or attorney/paralegal. Compromise appears to be part of the nature of most attorneys—it is an essential tool for anyone attempting to negotiate the resolution of a legal case—so most are quite amenable to its use in resolving office conflicts.

Compromise avoids some of the problems of the two approaches we have discussed so far. The conflict is acknowledged and a resolution is found that may leave both parties feeling they got something, as opposed to accommodation in which one party simply satisfies the interests of the other. It is especially helpful when a quick, acceptable solution is needed as opposed to a "right" solution that will take too long or require too many resources to attain.

On the downside, it does mean giving up something also. It can become a habit with the two parties always feeling pressure to meet in the middle because they did so in the past—even when the issue is really important to them. It is appropriate when half a loaf is indeed better than none. If each of you needs a ten-foot ladder, a compromise that leaves both with five feet of that ladder does neither of you good. In fact, since both parties are left unsatisfied, it doubles the downside of the accommodation approach.

The inclination to compromise can sometimes sell both parties short in another way. As mentioned previously, many of the conflicts between paralegals and attorneys are only apparent conflicts. With open and honest communication between them, they would be mindful that they share the same goal, maximization of the contributions that each of them bring to the legal team. If they jump to a compromise a valuable opportunity for communication and understanding may be lost. The conflict may be resolved, but potential solutions that would accomplish their joint goals are never considered. It is easy to understand, given the time pressures of legal practice, how tempting a quick and easy compromise comes to mind as the primary means of dealing with such conflicts. However, devoting a bit more time and thought to the concerns underlying the conflict would likely lead to worthwhile benefits to the attorney, the paralegal and the legal team as a whole.

- *Competition.* This is seldom a good option for paralegals dealing with their attorney. There may be times when important issues are on the line and you feel you simply must come out on top, but you have to realize that you may be an unemployed winner. Since many attorneys are competitive, it is especially important for you to be self-aware of your own approach. It is hard to envision an attorney and paralegal working well as a legal team if they are competitive *with each other.* If your attorney approaches conflict competitively, it is especially important that you attempt to adopt another approach and steer the conflict resolution process in another direction.

- *Collaboration.* This is also referred to as the "problem solving" approach. It is especially useful when those involved in a conflict will have to work together as you and your attorney will. However, it generally requires more time, attention and thought than the other approaches. Generally people approach conflict as if it always involved splitting that loaf of bread when quite frequently that is not the case. Remember that ten-foot ladder. Dividing it in two did neither party any good. Taking turns using it would allow both of you to climb to the top. As members of a legal team, the attorney and paralegal are likely to be collaborative and work together to solve problems as a matter of course. Yet, all too often, they fail to apply the methods they use to solving the problems of others to solving their own problems.

Collaboration requires that both parties be honest about their real concerns and open to hearing the real concerns of the other side. Since it is often difficult for one or both parties to identify and articulate their own real concerns, each has to be especially attuned to the permutations of the other's statements. For example, disputes over wages or salary are often really about a feeling on the part of the paralegal that her worth is not being acknowledged and a feeling on the part of the attorney that the paralegal is insufficiently aware of the economic realities of running a law office. If the real concerns can be identified, the parties can collaborate on a resolution that addresses those concerns. Such resolutions are more satisfying to all participants and are likely to lead to more permanent resolutions and better long term relationships.

Awareness of the various approaches to resolving conflict, your attorney's general approach and your own general approach can help resolve conflicts before they becomes major problems. Except for avoidance, which is seldom helpful for any conflict of significant import, each approach requires communication, so in the next section we will turn to that topic.

E. Establishing Lines of Communication

Communication is important throughut the attorney/paralegal relationship, not just in resolving conflict. Good communication can prevent many, if not most, of those conflicts from arising. But good communication is also necessary in every aspect of the legal team's relationship and operations. The successful legal team must be effective and efficient. You must be able to obtain understandable instructions and supervision from your attorney and be able to communicate the results of your work to her. You each must be able to communicate your expectations of each other and your ability to meet the expectations of the other.

Communication requires both the ability to deliver information well and to listen well. Information must be delivered not only clearly but in a way that the listener can accept, interpret and respond. Frequently misunderstandings arise because we assume that our listeners are hearing what we say in the same context, with the same emotional baggage, the same basic connotation of the words and so on as we have. When we have something important to say, we assume that the importance will be self-evident and engage the listener's attention by it's very content. In the end, if we want to be heard and understood, we must take responsibility for seeing that the information is heard and understood rather than simply delivered. If we want real communication, we must also be responsible listeners.

Chances are you are already aware that communication skills are an essential part of a paralegal's repertoire. The topic is usually covered in an introductory course for paralegal study. Those skills should also be brought to bear when communicating with your attorney keeping in mind what you know about attorneys in general and your attorney in particular including his management style and approaches to conflict. This is especially important when attempting to obtain understandable instructions from the attorney and when instructing the attorney as discussed below.

Although the importance of communication skills for the paralegal is emphasized in almost every paralegal education, what it means to have those skills is not always made clear. Before proceeding, then, we will take a brief review

of the standard aspects of good communication in the context of the parale-
gal/attorney relationship:

- Be aware of things that may stand in the way of your attorney hearing what
  you have to say, for example:
  - Lack of attention. As stated above, your attorney is likely to be under
    a great deal of pressure and have a lot going on. While they really want
    to be focused on what you are saying, their minds may be partially
    otherwise occupied.
  - The attorney generally has prior experience with both the law and em-
    ployees, and the experience may be quite different from yours. She
    may jump to conclusions or make unwarranted assumptions about
    what you are saying rather than truly hearing what you are saying, es-
    pecially if she is in a hurry.
  - The reverse side of the coin is that the attorney may have little expe-
    rience with paralegals and therefore not have an understanding of
    some things that you assume the attorney knows.
  - You may simply have different perceptions regarding the topic of
    communication, especially if you there is a significant gap between
    your ages.
- Be aware of non-verbal messages, both the ones you receive from the attorney and the one you are giving. If your body language does not line
  up with what you are saying, you may add to confusion rather than minimize it. Facial expressions, especially around the eyes, and hand move-
  ments are the primary places to look for communication signals, but
  posture can also be revealing.
- Be clear. Think about what you want to say before you say it. Don't be
  afraid to make and bring notes or a checklist of important points for reference during the conversation. Know why you are having the conversation and what you hope to bring away from it before beginning.
- Avoid being confrontational, complaining or discourteous. You are seeking communication. Be aware not only of what you say, but how you
  sound.
- Be concise. Again, thinking ahead and making a checklist may help. Keep
  your conversation on point. Digressions are distracting and waste time.
- Be direct and accurate. If you intend to rely on specific information, ver-
  ify the information before you start the discussion.
- Pause and assess the response to what you have said.
  - Watch for body language signals.
  - Listen to what the other person says without interruption. You can-
    not assess the impact of what you have said if you do not listen openly.

- ○ Ask questions to make sure you have been correctly understood.
  - ○ Ask yourself whether *you* are making unwarranted assumptions about the listener's understanding and the listener's response.
- Be as positive and non-critical as possible. Express concerns in terms of yourself rather in terms that are critical of the listener. For example, "I need more instruction" and "You don't give me enough instruction" both express the same thought, but the former is more likely to obtain the result you want.
- Make eye contact with the attorney. Speak to her, not to the floor, your lap, your notes or the window behind her.
- Handle criticism with dignity and professionalism. Look for the positive side of any criticism, even when the person doing the criticism does not appear to have any positive intent. Be aware that your own (that is, everyone's) instinctive reaction to criticism is to become defensive and "fight back." You can only learn from criticism or justifiably reject it if you have listened to it openly and assessed it honestly.
- Smile.

Obtaining Understandable Instructions and Instructing the Attorney

The keys to an effective, sustainable attorney/paralegal relationship include respect for each other's role on the legal team and communication about and within those roles. As we already discussed you can greatly improve the respect you receive from your attorney through professional conduct and high quality work (as opposed to just satisfactory work.) We also discussed, however, the confusion that may exist over the role of the paralegal. That confusion results not only in a less effective legal team, but in frustration and unhappiness on the part of both the attorney and paralegal.

You can help reduce the confusion by being aware of the potential for it, being clear in your own mind about what you can and cannot do, and being willing to talk to your attorney about it in an open, honest and non-confrontational way. This is especially true in obtaining the instructions you need to do your job correctly.

No one benefits from you spending four hours completing a research project only to find out you did not understand what the attorney was asking. Nor is it beneficial to spend four hours completing a project you do understand if a few clarifying questions would have made it a one hour project. On the other hand, receiving highly detailed instructions or only unchallenging tasks that require little or no instruction wastes the attorney's time, under-utilizes you as a paralegal which wastes the attorney's money and your competence and leads to frustration on your part, if not his.

However, it is not likely that he did this intentionally. More likely, he was simply unaware that more was needed, either because that is his management style, he made faulty assumptions or he has an insufficient understanding of what you in particular or paralegals in general can do. He cannot read your mind, and you cannot read his.

So you can see that obtaining proper instructions means instructing the attorney. We come back again to basic communication. Assuming you have established or are establishing yourself as a professional in the office, we can look at the steps for preventing and resolving these difficulties, based on what you have learned in this chapter:

- Listen to, or read, what you receive from your attorney carefully. Many times misunderstanding arises because the paralegal, who is also often under pressure and time constraints reads hurriedly and makes assumptions. If you receive your assignment from the attorney orally, take notes. If you receive it via email, remember that it may have been written hurriedly by the attorney. Either way, she may very well not have thought through all the permutations herself.
    - Ask yourself whether what you have received from the attorney could be interpreted more than one way.
    - Ask yourself what you are being asked to do and what you need to do about it.
    - Ask yourself whether you have the competence to complete the assigned task without assistance.
- Take the time to identify exactly what is unclear to you or what help you need, so you can be clear and concise in your discussion with the attorney.
- Identify what additional information your attorney may need to understand your basic concern. Be prepared to explain not only what you need, but the additional information your attorney needs.
- Take the time to ask yourself how best to approach your attorney about a given topic based on the topic, the attorney's management style, the attorney's personality, and so on.
- Overcome the natural hesitancy to admit to your attorney that you need clarification or assistance.
- Get your attorney's attention. While sometimes both initial instructions and clarifications can only be done on the run as an attorney flies out the door to the courthouse, most of the time you can go to his office and ask for time to discuss your assignment. Make it clear that you are ask-

ing for *time*, "I have a few questions about the Will you want me to draft for Mr. Jones. Do you have some time for me now?" Or, "I can probably help you in drafting wills more than I have been. Do you have time to talk about where and how I can do more for you?" If she does not have time, set a time when she does.

- Be direct and to the point. Even if she does have time, she does not have a lot of it. Whether you are there to get more instruction on dealing with a particular client, or to explain how you can be a more productive member of the legal team, this is not the time to talk about other matters. Remember to have your checklist. Take notes.
- Be positive. You are there as a professional ensuring that you are getting what you need to do your job because you want to do the best possible job that can be done. That is a *good* thing. The attorney is more likely to understand that if *your* approach is a positive one, not one of criticism, complaint or whining.
- *Believe* in yourself and the communication you are making. Show him that belief in your body language as well as in what you say. Make eye contact while speaking.
- Rephrase in your own words what your understanding is and ask him if your understanding is correct.
- Ask questions to validate that you have understood each other.
- End the conversation when you have a sufficient understanding, unless the attorney continues the conversation.
- End the conversation by expressing your appreciation for her time and her help.

F. Dealing with a Difficult Attorney

Everything we have discussed so far will help when dealing with any attorney. However, there are some attorneys, who are, after-all, simply difficult people to deal with. There are no perfect solutions to this situation, especially since any employer can be difficult in so many ways: they can be rude, intimidating, control freaks or disengaged, vague and weak with no management skills or interest at all. If they have gotten to where they are like this, there is little likelihood you will change them. Instead, you will have to accommodate yourself to them (which is not to say you must always accommodate them). You may find the these suggestions helpful:

- Do outside reading on the type of person your attorney is so you have a better understanding of how to work for him and with him, whether he is a non-manager, a micro-manager or in between.
- Do not become engaged in control battles with your attorney. Do be clear with them about what your expectations and capabilities are, but do not resort to manipulation, passive-aggressive behavior and the like. In the end you may simply need to find a new employer. You want to leave on your own terms and not with a bad reference based on constant conflict between you and the attorney.
- Document clearly with friendly confirming emails your discussions with the attorney.
- Remain professional regardless of how they act.
- React unemotionally. Remember when they are loud, critical and rude, that it is they who has the problem not you. Refuse to engage.
- Do not engage in office gossip about your attorney. Everyone else either knows how he is based on their own experience with him or they do not know. Those that do know need not hear it from you. Those that do not know will likely not believe you. Both will think less of you as a result of your gossiping.
- Focus on discussion rather than confrontation when dealing with the attorney.
- Even bad employers have good days (or good moments during a day). Encourage this by acknowledging and praising it. Tell the micro-manager, "Thank you for letting me handle that on my own. I appreciate the trust you placed in me and I'm proud of how I was able to handle the situation."
- Leave the employer at work. It is great to relieve the stress by discussing it with your significant other or your best friend. It is also great to get validation from them. But avoid continuous fretting and stress over your employer at home. You need a break from it, and making it part of your home life will diminish that life as well as the work portion of your day.
- Set limits. You will need to have a back-up plan for this, that is, another job or a way of getting by until you can find one. But the fact is that you cannot tolerate a truly intolerably situation forever. At some point you need to determine what is unacceptable to you and make that clear to your attorney. Professionally, uncritically, unemotionally and with even tone set and state your limits: "I do not work well when I am yelled at. Please speak normally to me." "I cannot accept your phone calls at home." "I cannot do a good job without instructions. Please clarify this for me." Be prepared to change employment if your limits, once set and stated, are repeatedly breached.

G. Ethical Considerations

You might think that the paralegal/attorney relationship, being somewhat personal in nature, would not entail much by way of formal ethical discussion beyond the work ethic and personal confidentiality we have already discussed in this chapter. However, that relationship can be the source of some of the most difficult ethical decisions a paralegal has to make: What do I do if I know my attorney is violating the Rules of Ethical Conduct and/or a law? And, even worse, what do I do if my attorney asks me to do something unethical?

The rules of professional conduct for attorneys in all states have some form of rule that requires attorneys to report unethical conduct by another attorney to the proper authority. There is much discussion about these rules in terms of exactly what conduct requires disclosure, how certain the attorney must be of the violation before reporting it, whether the attorney must only reveal the information if asked or must take the positive step of reporting even if not asked.

The attorneys' rules of professional conduct are not directly binding upon you, but they can still act as a guide as to what the right course of action is for you. If you become aware of ethical violations by *another* attorney, you should bring it to the attention of your attorney and let her handle it. Document the fact that you brought it to your attorney's attention and asked for direction. But doing the correct thing is not so easy if it is your attorney who you believe is engaging or has engaged in unethical conduct.

Fortunately, you can find some guidance in the ethical codes of various paralegal associations. Recall that earlier we discussed the importance of you, as a professional, belonging to one or more of these associations and participating in their listservs, reading their journals and the like. It will be helpful for you to discuss these types of issues (in a way that preserves confidentiality) with other members of those associations. The ethical codes of these organizations are not laws, but they do provide a good framework for you to use in facing these difficult issues.

We will not review all such codes, but it is helpful here to review at least one. The National Federation of Paralegal Associations has adopted a Model Code that contains two provisions relating to this topic. One, EC 1-2(f) requires that the proper authority be informed of any client trust fund violations. The other, EC 1-3(d) similarly requires reporting any "fraud, deceit, or dishonesty."

Of course, neither of these rules applies to information that is subject to the overall rules of attorney/client confidentiality, but if the conduct about which you are concerned is your own attorney's conduct, it is not likely to involve that privilege. And some common sense must be invoked in interpreting the language of the code. The attorney asking you to tell a client he is in court when he is really in his office is dishonest, but is not likely to rise to the level requiring (or even suggesting) reporting.

As stated above, these codes do not have the force of law. In particular situation you may want to seek legal advice yourself. Some states do have laws making failure to report certain actions, such as judicial bribery, a crime. However, for the most part, it is really of a matter of ethics rather than legal consequence for the paralegal (unlike an attorney who can lose his license). In most cases it is going to be a matter of balancing your personal interest (you will likely lose your job if for no other reason than the attorney may lose his license) with your personal integrity, protecting the public and maintaining the integrity of the legal profession. In the end, I would hope that personal integrity wins out over personal interests, but you must be the judge in each situation.

If you do decide to report, I suggest obtaining legal advice first from an attorney outside of the office in which you work. Remember that attorney has a firm obligation to keep what you tell her confidential. That attorney can advise you regarding protections to which you may be entitled, the proper authority to which you should report and the correct procedures for reporting. Generally, you will receive immunity from being sued by your employer for slander and libel, and you may be entitled to certain protections against on-the-job retaliation under "Whistleblower" laws. She will help you analyze the situation to determine whether you have the necessary facts and have properly interpreted them, and she will validate your decision regarding the proper balancing of interest and integrity. Again, other members of your paralegal professional association may be helpful in locating the best attorney for this purpose.

Conclusion

Any employer/employee relationship, indeed any relationship, will have its high and low points, and the attorney/paralegal relationship is no exception. Like other relationships, the attorney/paralegal relationship works best when it is based on mutual respect, mutual understanding and good communication. Unlike many other relationships, the attorney/paralegal relationship is a relationship between professionals, so there is an inherent basis for mutual respect, understanding and communication.

You can best manage that relationship by maintaining high professional standards for yourself, doing your best to understand the attorney, and help the attorney understand you and your role in the legal team through open and

honest communication. This chapter has provided you with the basic knowledge and techniques to do this.

The payback for your efforts can be enormous. There is little in life, especially the work portion of life, as gratifying as being part of an effective, efficient, successful legal team comprised in part of a paralegal and an attorney with
a good working relationship.

Chapter Seven

Managing Your Litigation— Crucial Tools for Building a Better Trial

The paralegal's role in building a better trial requires all the traditional paralegal skills: interpersonal skills, effective communication, research, writing and the like. Likewise, the skills discussed in this book must be applied: managing time, work, files, clients and attorney/paralegal relationships. In this chapter we'll apply all of these skills using some tools crucial to building a better trial.

A. Trial Tactics

One key to managing your relationship with your attorney is a mutual understanding of what each of you does as part of the legal team. Understanding your attorney's use of trial tactic is also an essential tool for assisting in building a better trial with that attorney. Often the paralegal is frustrated because, after hours of research and preparation, the attorney does not seem to be applying the resulting work to the trial. However, trials are more than just the application of rules of procedure, rules of evidences, statutes and case law to a set of facts.

Just as important as knowing the rules and law is knowing *how* and *when* to employ them in the context of a particular trial. While knowledge of the rules of evidence will tell the attorney she *can object* to a question, she must use your preparation and her judgment to determine *whether* to object. At each opportunity to object she must determine instantly:

- whether an objection is likely to succeed because an unsuccessful objection may create the wrong impression in the jury's mind;
- whether repeated objections, even if successful, will cause a jury to think her client has something to hide;

- whether a successful objection will later prejudice her ability to use similar evidence favorable to her case;

and many other potential ramifications.

The trial attorney must make tactical use of all the weapons available. This can only be done if the case is thoroughly prepared; the facts, law and rules all known and the evidence all available. There are several excellent books devoted to effective trial tactics, a topic which cannot be covered comprehensively here. However, there are several general tactical considerations which will be helpful to you in understanding what your attorney is doing and how you can most effectively assist the attorney.

Searching for Truth in All the Wrong Places

Trials are often described as forums in which everyone searches for truth with truth ultimately being attained in the form of a jury verdict. However, the jury's verdict is based on the evidence presented to it and that evidence may vary dramatically from what actually happened. Not all evidence is welcomed (admissible) at a trial under the Rules of Evidence. Not all evidence has the same relevance. Not all evidence has the same effectiveness. Not all evidence is presented in a way that the jury can understand.

Facts, evidence and proof are not the same. Many clients do not understand the difference. As discussed in Chapter Six, a well-informed client is the easiest to manage and most able to be an effective member of the legal team. You will often find it necessary to explain the differences between facts, evidence and proof and how each of them relates to the case. This requires a rudimentary understanding of legal underpinnings of the case itself: "causes of action" and "elements."

Each case involves one or more "causes of action." For example, a case involving the sale of a defective product may have causes of action for breach of contract, breach of express warranty and breach of implied warranty. A case for defective construction of a home may have a cause of action for breach of contract, breach of statutory requirements, negligence and legal doctrines such as unjust enrichment.

Each of these causes of action has its own "elements," that is, things that must be proved. An action for breach of contract requires showing a valid contract was formed, i.e., (a) there was an offer, (b) an acceptance and (c) consideration passed (d) between two or more parties with legal capacity, (e) and the transaction itself was legal. Generally, only evidence that tends to prove or disprove one of those elements is admissible in court. You may recall these explanations from Chapter Five where we discussed them in the context of informing your client as part of the legal team, but they bear another look in this context.

Facts of a case are the bits and pieces that comprise what happened —the event which brought the parties to court—such as the particularities of the automobile accident, the assault, the boundary dispute or the contract dispute. For example, it may be a fact of an automobile accident case that one went through an intersection when the traffic light in his direction was red. However, this "fact" may be contested by the parties. One party will say the light was red and the other party will say it was green.

Evidence is something that tends to show, confirm or verify a fact. It can be testimony such as the driver testifying he looked at the light before he entered the intersection. Not all evidence is equally convincing. Testimony from an un-involved third party, i.e., a school crossing guard, that the light was red or green, may be more convincing than the testimony of the driver of either car involved in the accident. A picture taken by a camera set up to track drivers' speed may be even more convincing.

From the lawyer's perspective, evidence is more important than actual facts. Cases must be evaluated and presented based on the evidence available for presentation rather than on the facts the attorney believes is true. We are more concerned about what can be proven than simply what occurred. We can assure our clients that we believe the doctor told them they would never be the same, but must make them understand that what matters is what the doctor says in his reports and on the witness stand.

Proof is simply whatever evidence is sufficient to convince a jury to accept a fact as true. Thus, a driver's testimony that the light was green when she went through the intersection is proof if it is credible enough for the jury to accept it as a true statement of the facts, and is not proof if the jury does not accept it.

We discussed the need to explain such legal concepts to clients in Chapter Five and will discuss the use of these concepts more in this chapter especially as they come into play in the trial notebook. For now we will focus on considerations that flow from the fact that the legal team is not necessarily searching for "the truth." Rather it is searching for the best evidence and the best way to present that evidence to convince a jury that it is proof of facts that establish the elements of the causes(s) of action at issue in the legal action.

Since the search for evidence begins when the case starts, trial tactics considerations start during, or even before, the initial client interview, as we mentioned in Chapter Five. From the start:

- *Know the elements of your case* and what you need both theoretically and practically to prove each one of them. (More on this when we discuss litigation and trial notebooks.)
- Make your client part of your legal team by explaining the process to her in terms she can understand.
- Develop an investigation and discovery plan designed around the elements of your case.
- Be aware of the problems with evidence.
  - No piece of evidence is "proof positive."
  - Any piece of evidence can be made to look other than it is.
  - Every piece of evidence is influenced by how it came into existence, how it has been handled and how it has been/is being perceived by the parties, witnesses, attorneys, judge and jury (each of whom bring their own pre-conceptions to the courtroom).
  - Often *how* evidence is presented is as important as what evidence is presented.

Presentation Counts — The Best Dog & Pony Show Wins

Evidence becomes proof when it convinces a jury. Regardless of the intrinsic value of the evidence, it is not convincing unless the jury hears or sees it, understands it and is persuaded by it. When planning what evidence to present and how to present it, step out of your role as a paralegal and try to assume the role of a juror. This is tricky. It's not enough to say "How would this appear to *me* if *I* were a juror on this case." The jurors on your case are not likely to have any legal education or have any knowledge of the case, as you have.

We'll talk more about knowing your jury, but even before the jury pool is formed, weeks earlier when you and your attorney are planning your evidence presentation, you must try to view your evidence from the stand point of your likely jurors. The same evidence may be viewed differently by a Manhattan jury than by a jury in rural Arkansas. Try to understand the mindset of your likely jurors and present the evidence in a way that is likely to be heard by, remembered by, and persuasive to *those* jurors.

Demonstrative Aids and Exhibits

Remember some people learn best through audio, but these days most people are visually oriented. Therefore, demonstrative aids are more important than ever. An x-ray is much more effective than a doctor's description of a broken bone. An x-ray combined with the doctor's description is better yet. Photographs of an intersection are better than testimony about the intersection. Damages itemized on a flip chart or slides are more likely to be remembered than your client's testimony about those damages.

Younger juries may react better to animated demonstrative aids. My kids delight in telling me how only old people are impressed by PowerPoint presentations. Young people want video clips and sound. This is probably true, but older jurors may be more appreciative of aids that go at a slower pace.

In general, keep in mind that more and bigger are not necessarily better. Use demonstrative aids to emphasize important points—those you want to impress upon the jurors' minds. If you use them to illustrate every point, they do not assist the jurors in remembering what is and what is not important. They become a jumble of sense impressions, more confusing than clarifying.

Finally, keep in mind the fine line between a *professional* presentation and one that appears *slick*. Jurors respect presentations and presenters that respect them. While much of what is done at a trial is designed to manipulate the jury's minds and hearts, it must be done without the jurors feeling manipulated.

Dress for Success

This does not mean "look successful." It's my way of saying you have to be aware that the jury is not just looking at the evidence as presented; it is looking at the presenters of the evidence.

Consider a real circus dog and pony show; the performer and the atmosphere are at least as important as the acts performed. This principle applies to almost any performance meant to leave an impression or make a point on an audience. Every political operative considers not just what is being said, but the backdrop for the speech. Rock stars don't just sing—they perform. The jury is your attorney's audience. They are watching and waiting for the show.

Like most performers, your legal team is "on" every moment the jurors are in the jury box (and when they are entering or leaving the box). They are watching not just the witness on the stand and the attorney examining the witness, but also the rest of the "performance."

In this respect it *is* important how the performers dress and appear to the jury. The performers include the attorney, the paralegal, the client and the witnesses. Each of you most dress appropriately for your role, keeping in mind that you must dress *for the jury*. Even jurors who seem to be paying little attention seem to notice clothing—distracting ties, short skirts, body-piercing and tattoos. If a client is pleading poverty, she cannot show up day after day in $300 dollar outfits, dazzling jewelry, $30 nails and $50 hair. An expert witness will not impress a jury if he dresses unprofessionally. In fact, he should dress for *the jury's conception of his* profession—a doctor as a doctor, a contractor as a contractor and a professor as a professor.

Remind clients and witnesses that they are subject to observation by the jury anytime jurors are present. A jury will assume that a client who is rude to or snarls at the other party, was equally rude and disagreeable during the event or events that led the parties to court, regardless of how that client or witness presents on the stand. In fact, a client or witness who acts differently on the stand than when he thinks the jury isn't watching is telling the jury not to believe him, as his presentation on the stand is not the "true" him.

Jurors generally do not react favorably to clients who mumble "that's a lie" under their breath or gasp and shake their heads in reaction to a witness' testimony. Clients who squirm, constantly adjust their clothes (this happens a lot with clients who are not used to wearing a tie and who "dress up" just for the trial), or fidget nervously may look as though they have something to hide.

Be Prepared

In many respects trial preparation is the most important aspect of a successful trial. No matter how good a case is, it is likely to lose if the legal team is not prepared to present it and counter the other side's presentation. Often it is the best prepared case that wins, not the best case.

Trial preparation goes beyond preparing exhibits, witness subpoenas and opening statements. The exhibits are not helpful if you can't find them at trial when they are needed. Witnesses can actually be harmful if the attorney does not understand what they add to the presentation and how to extract that value from them in a way the jury will understand and remember.

All of the information necessary to present the case in a winning way must be organized in a way that allows for easy and immediate retrieval. It must be cross-referenced, indexed and available. This will be discussed more in the section on trial notebooks.

Yet even this is not enough. Your legal team should be prepared in a way that leaves as little as possible to chance. The team should know not only the case, but also the judge, the jury, the courtroom, the witnesses and the parties.

The Judge. Is the judge conservative or liberal on issues affecting the admissibility of evidence? What are the judge's expectations regarding pre-trial briefs, draft jury instructions, making a record, managing time, managing witnesses and the other details of trial management? If you or your attorney have not appeared before the judge before, take the time to watch the judge in action a week or so before your trial. If this can't be done, use your network to find out as much as possible about the judge *before* your attorney enters the courtroom.

The Jury. Different jurisdictions have different rules and procedures regarding the information provided about jurors. The legal team must know those rules and procedures and use them. In addition, the team will have many opportunities to observe the jurors both before and after the selection of your jury. Since you and the attorney both have other responsibilities, you should share this one. Often you can be the attorney's eyes and ears, watching the body language of the potential jurors while she is conducting *voir dire* of a particular juror. How are they reacting to the questions? How do they look at your client? How do they react to the other attorney? How interested do they appear? The more that is known about the jury, the more the presentation can be keyed to that jury.

The Witnesses and the Parties. Frequently trial preparations focus on what the witnesses or parties are going to say. The well-prepared legal team will also consider everything they can about the witnesses themselves. In the witness section of the trial notebook, include a short biography of the witness or party and notes about impressions obtained by the attorney, you or investigators during interviews or depositions. Again, much additional information can be obtained during the trial through observation. This is another opportunity for you to be the attorney's second set of eyes and ears.

The Courtroom. Check out the courtroom in advance. Where can the flip chart stands be placed to maximize visibility by witnesses, the judge and the jury at the same time? Where can you plug in the projector? How much room and light are available? Will you need an additional table? How can you leave the counsel table to contact the next witness with the least distraction? Where will the witnesses sit while waiting their turn to testify?

Your goal is a professional presentation. The power of the Power-Point presentation on damages during closing argument is greatly diminished if you and the attorney find there is no way to position the equipment so that it can be plugged in, even if the court allows time so an extension cord can be found.

Prepare the Client

Preparing the client requires more than just reviewing their testimony. Most clients will have never been through the litigation process, much less have been the star of a trial presentation. (Even if the client does not testify in a criminal case, he is the star and watched carefully by the jury.) The client's nervousness, confusion and uncertainty will adversely affect his demeanor and his testimony. Much of that effect can be avoided by making the client familiar with the process and the courtroom itself.

Bring the client to the courthouse and the courtroom in advance. Show him where he will sit; where the judge, jury, clerk, stenographer, bailiffs and so on will be located. Explain the role of each of the people who will be in the courtroom. Show him the path for walking from the counsel table to the witness box. Let him sit in the box and see the courtroom from that perspective. Show him where the attorneys will stand while questioning him. Show him where to get water and where the restrooms are.

A short trip to the courtroom in advance can change a client's entire attitude. Since he does not have to worry and wonder about these details, he can focus on his role, his testimony and the overall presentation. He may actually become helpful to the process, but at least he'll not require as much of your attention during the trial.

Establish a Theme — Tell a Story

Your attorney will not simply be presenting the evidence. He'll be telling the jury his client's story. In most cases, his client will be the hero of the story and the other party will be the villain. This can be confusing to a jury because at the same time the other attorney is telling her client's story. In that story her client is the hero and yours is the villain. Thus, many trial tactics are designed to narrow and simplify the story.

Just like a good story teller, your attorney will want to establish a theme for the trial. In her story, your client is a hard working man so traumatized by his wife's filing for divorce he's unable to work, and the other client is a gold-digger who has never been interested in anything but the client's money. In the other attorney's story, her client has given up her own career to build her husband's career, only to be cut-off from the benefits of his career when the marriage fell apart. Judgments such as what evidence to use and when to use it or which witnesses to call and what to ask them will be made based on how the evidence or witnesses' testimonies add or detract from the theme.

The story and theme must fit your client and your client must be made aware of this theme, how he fits into it and how he fits into the story telling process. The objective cannot be to mold the client or the facts to the story, so the story must be one that "fits" the client and the facts, and will be effective with the jury. You can't turn the snarling grizzly bear of a client into a teddy bear for trial. As we mentioned before, the jury will have ample opportunity to see through the smiling veneer to the snarling client. However, once the theme is set, your client will be most helpful if she understands what is being projected to the jury.

Your attorney's story will likely come with a "hook." The hook often takes the form of phrases (often alliterative) repeated many times during the trial. You may recall the way "If the glove does not fit, you must acquit" was used during the O.J. Simpson murder trial. Or the hook may be certain lines of questioning that appear during examination of every witness as well as in the opening statement and closing argument. Perhaps the car accident victim is attempting to blame everything bad about his life on the accident. He refuses to accept personal responsibility for *anything.* The attorney may focus on the jury's own sense of personal responsibility, pointing out that the "victim" blames the police for not fully investigating the accident, the ER personnel for an incomplete record, his doctor for not recognizing the extent of his problem, and his physical therapist for not writing down his complaints.

Often the jury will not remember the intricate details of a doctor's report, but they will remember "the hook." In an effort to keep the story simple but powerful, your attorney may ignore complicated and confusing evidence that appears to be important, in favor of evidence with less importance but more impact.

Sitting Down and Shutting-Up

Sometimes your attorney makes the best presentation by doing nothing. This is not a comment on your attorney's abilities, but recognition that there are times when the presentation is best enhanced by refraining from action rather than by taking action.

As discussed above, repeated objections, even if successful, may cause a jury to think her client has something to hide. Here are a few other examples when it may be better not to act:

- The witness is rambling and the rambling makes the witness appear incoherent or unreliable;

- The objectionable testimony opens the door to issues on cross examination that would otherwise be off limits;
- Questioning of a witness is likely to cause confusion on an issue that is fairly clear;
- Questioning of a witness will bore the jury, causing the jurors to stop paying attention;
- Questioning of a witness, especially a very young, vulnerable or distraught witness, will cause the attorney to look like a bully (a characterization that may be transferred to the attorney's client); and
- The attorney does not know the answer to the question, or likely the answers will be harmful to the case.

This is an area in which you can be especially helpful in your role as a second set of eyes and ears for the attorney. While the attorney is focused on questioning a witness, for example, you can be watching the judge and jury for reactions and give the attorney feedback which can be used to determine when and whether to ask additional questions.

Trial Tactics and Strategy Start at the Initial Client Interview

Although most cases settle without trial, each case must be treated from the beginning as if it will go to trial. Indeed, the best way to avoid a trial is for the other side to recognize just how well-prepared your team is to conduct one if necessary. So we'll end this section by looking back at some of the points made at the beginning of the section. From the initial client interview on:

- *Know the elements of your case* and what you need both theoretically and practically to prove each one of them.
- Develop an investigation and discovery plan designed around the elements of your case.
- Be aware of the problems with evidence.
  - No piece of evidence is "proof positive."
  - Any piece of evidence can be made to look other than it is.
  - Every piece of evidence is influenced by how it came into existence, how it has been handled and how it has been/is being perceived by the parties, witness, attorneys, judge and jury (each of whom bring their own pre-conceptions to the courtroom.)
  - Often *how* evidence is presented is as important as what evidence is presented

- Perhaps most important, make your client part of your legal team by explaining the process to her in terms she can understand.

B. Litigation Notebooks

The best evidence, the best testimony and the best legal research are of little use at trial unless they are available at trial and they can be easily produced and effectively used. The trial notebook makes this possible. A well organized, indexed and cross-referenced trial notebook can actually make the difference between winning and losing a case. However, the process starts when the file is first opened. From the beginning, the litigation itself should be organized around the elements of the causes of action.

As stated in the previous section, each case involves one or more causes of action. Each of these causes of action has its own elements, that is, things that must be proved. As the client initially recounts the events which brought her into your attorney's office, you and the attorney will begin to sort her account into possible causes of action—contract, negligence, breach of warranty and so on. You or the attorney will ask for additional information based on these possible causes of action.

The total body of information will be used to determine whether the facts stated by your client will satisfy the elements of each cause of action. The complaint and the entire litigation process will then be designed around those elements. You will seek evidence through further interviews, investigation and discovery, which tends to prove or disprove the necessary elements.

Thus, as we discussed a bit earlier from the start of each case, the legal team must

- *Know the elements of the case* and what is needed both theoretically and practically to prove each one of them.
- Make your client part of the legal team by explaining the process to him in terms he can understand.
- Develop an investigation and discovery plan designed around the elements of your case.

The results of all this work is best maintained in a litigation notebook. In fact, there may be a set of notebooks organized for motion practice, discovery, evidence and ultimately trial. Each of these notebooks should be organized in terms of the facts available as evidence to prove the elements of the case, and they should follow these simple steps:

Step 1: State the Cause(s) of Action.

Any attempt to analyze and utilize evidence—or the litigation process itself—must start with a clear understanding of the causes of action (civil litigation) or charges (criminal litigation). Therefore, the notebook should start with a statement of the cause of action or charge as it relates to the facts of your case. For example, if someone is being sued for injuries incurred in a car accident, the cause of action might be stated as "Defendant caused plaintiff injury by negligent operation of an automobile, to wit: he failed to obey traffic control device (stop sign) resulting in a collision between his vehicle and plaintiff's vehicle." Each cause of action is a "trunk" for an "evidence tree," an organizational tools discussed in the next section.

Step 2: State the elements that must be proved.

In order to get by a motion for judgment as a matter of law and allow the jury to consider your case, you must submit evidence on each element of the pertinent cause of action or charge. Therefore, for each cause of action or charge, the next step is to set forth the elements. For example in a car accident, the elements may include (1) existence of a duty (obey traffic control devices), (2) failure to exercise that duty (failed to stop for stop sign) and (3) causing damage (physical injury or property damage to another party). In order to get a fair jury verdict, you must also show (4) the extent of that injury or damage.

Step 3: State the facts in your case that address each element.

You cannot be sure you are submitting evidence on each element unless you know what facts of your client's story fit each element and how they fit that element. In the car accident example, (1) the existence of a stop sign satisfies the first element (when supported by citation to the relevant statute), (2) the fact that defendant did not stop for the sign satisfies the second element and so on.

Step 4: State the evidence available that supports each fact.

The existence of a stop sign cannot be assumed, it must be "proven." In this example, you might prove the existence of the stop sign through testimony of your client, the police officer called to the scene, the ambulance driver, the person who lives in the house at the intersection corner or photographs. List all sources of evidence of each fact.

Step 5: State the foundation needed to get the evidence admitted unless it is obvious.

In order to get the neighbor's testimony in you are going to have to establish where he lives, whether he has observed the intersection, when he last saw the stop sign in place and similar foundational facts.

Step 6: State possible objections to the evidence.

For example, a defense attorney might object to testimony from the person who lives at the intersection because the last time he saw the sign up was the previous night before he went to sleep and does not know whether it has been knocked down or removed by vandals during the night. State the rule(s) which the attorney would use to make the objection, e.g., Rule 403 (Relevance) or 602 (Lack of Personal Knowledge).

Step 7: State responses to possible objections with reference to the appropriate rule and pertinent case law.

In the above example, the plaintiff's attorney might argue that the evidence gets in under Rule 401 and jury can consider the weight of the testimony in light of the facts brought out by the defense on cross-examination.

Step 8: Cross reference your evidence to your Witness Summary Pages and Exhibit Pages.

If you are going to show the existence of the stop sign through your client, the police officer and the neighbor, list it on each of their summary pages. If you are going to show the extent of plaintiff's injuries through hospital bills and photographs from the scene of the accident, reference this for each exhibit in the exhibit index.

Trial Notebooks

Every successful litigation team has a method for organizing the information they will accumulate during the litigation process and utilize at trial. Judges and juries expect a lawyer not only to be prepared but to be organized. Every trial team should have a simple method that is effective for that team. The method of organizing the trial notebook will often depend on the type of case, office policy or the preference of your attorney. Most are organized around the trial process itself, beginning with pre-trial motions and ending with post-judgment motions. In between there may be sections for

- Jury selection (e.g., voir dire questions, information on prospective jurors, or legal research justifying likely challenges for cause)

- Opening statement
- Direct examination of witnesses
- Legal research and notes for motions at the end of plaintiff's evidence
- Cross examination of witnesses
- Exhibits
- Legal research and notes for motions at the end of defendant's evidence
- Closing arguments
- Jury Verdict Forms and Jury Instructions

Notebook dividers with pre-printed trial notebook sections are available from several companies.

Regardless of how the notebook is divided into sections, each section must be organized in a way that recognizes the essential goal of the trial—an effective presentation of your client's case in a way that convinces the jury of your client's position on each of the elements.

During this discussion I have used several concepts and phrases with which you may not be familiar so in the rest of this chapter we'll touch briefly on evidence trees, exhibit lists, witness lists, and witness preparation. In the conclusion, the importance of cross referencing will be emphasized.

Evidence Trees

We'll start by applying the organizational steps to a sample case and build a branch or two of an evidence tree. Let's work with a simple fact pattern encompassing some of the examples used above:

Your client, Hester Prynne, was injured during a collision with the defendant, Nathaniel Hawthorne. Nathaniel, traveling east on Main Street, failed to stop for a stop sign located at the corner of Main Street and High Street, and he collided with Hester, traveling south on High Street, in the intersection. There was no stop sign in Hester's direction of travel. Hester, who had no previous injuries, immediately felt severe pain in her lower back and her neck, and soon noticed blood on her forehead with an increasing headache. Hester believes Erin Dimmesdale, a woman who lives near the intersection, saw the accident. Hester believes someone, perhaps the police, perhaps someone from the newspaper, perhaps someone in the neighborhood, took pictures of the scene.

Step 1: State the Cause(s) of Action.

In this example, the cause of action is negligence and can be simply stated on Page One of the notebook:

> Defendant caused plaintiff injury by negligent operation of an automobile, to wit: he failed to obey traffic control device (stop sign) resulting in a collision between his vehicle and plaintiff's vehicle.

Step 2: State the Elements That Must Be Proved.

This statement of the cause of action is, however, only vaguely helpful for purposes of litigation. It may or may not be sufficient to withstand a motion to dismiss and certainly does not provide sufficient structure for designing an interview, investigation and discovery plan, or organizing and presenting evidence during trial. It is the trunk of the evidence tree, but lacks the branches on which the case will hang. We can provide the first, strong branches by listing the elements under the cause of action:

> **Prynne v. Hawthorne**
> **Cause of Action: Negligence**
> Defendant caused plaintiff injury by negligent operation of an automobile, to wit: he failed to obey traffic control device (stop sign) resulting in a collision between his vehicle and plaintiff's vehicle.
> Elements of Negligence Cause of Action:
> 1. Defendant was subject to a duty
> 2. Defendant breached his duty
> 3. Defendant's breach was the proximate cause
> 4. Resulting in injury to the Plaintiff

If we fail to introduce evidence on any one of these elements, our case will lose as a matter of law. If we fail to convince the jury on any one of these elements, we lose the case.

Step 3: State the facts in your case that address each element.

Having established the main branches, i.e., the elements, our tree can begin growing as we add the facts from our fact pattern that satisfy each of these elements.

> **Prynne v Hawthorne**
> **Cause of Action: Negligence**
> Defendant caused plaintiff injury by negligent operation of an automobile, to wit: he failed to obey traffic control device (stop sign) resulting in a collision between his vehicle and plaintiff's vehicle.
> Elements of Negligence Cause of Action:
> 1. Defendant was subject to a duty
>
>   **Facts:**
>   A. Defendant was traveling east on Main Street.
>   B. There was a posted stop sign at the intersection of Main and High Streets on the date of the accident.
>   C. There was no obstruction of Defendant's view of the stop sign

      D.   State law imposes a duty on motorists to stop for stop signs and yield the right of way to motorists traveling on intersecting highways.

  2. Defendant breached his duty

      Facts:

      A.   Defendant failed to stop for the stop sign.

  3. Defendant's breach was the proximate cause

      Facts:

      A.   Plaintiff was maintaining proper speed and paying attention to her driving.

  4. Resulting in injury to the Plaintiff

      Facts:

      A.   Plaintiff had no injuries prior to the accident.

      B.   Plaintiff immediately felt severe pain in her lower back and her neck, and soon noticed blood on her forehead with an increasing headache.

Step 4: State the evidence available that supports each fact.

The existence each of these "facts" cannot be assumed. Your legal team must produce evidence of each fact; evidence sufficient to convince the jury even if the other side contests that fact. At this point I suggest we move each element onto its own page.

Prynne v Hawthorne

Cause of Action: Negligence

Defendant caused plaintiff injury by negligent operation of an automobile, to wit: he failed to obey traffic control device (stop sign) resulting in a collision between his vehicle and plaintiff's vehicle.

Elements of Negligence Cause of Action:

1. Defendant was subject to a duty

      Facts:

      A.   Defendant was traveling east on Main Street.

         Evidence:

          i.   Plaintiff's testimony.

          ii.   Defendant's admission to police officer

          iii.   Witness Erin Dimmesdale's testimony

      B.   There was a posted stop sign at the intersection of Main and High Streets on the date of the accident.

         Evidence:

          i.   Plaintiff's testimony

          ii.   Police officer's testimony

          iii.   Witness Erin Dimmesdale's testimony

          iv.   Photographs of scene (Police? Newspaper? Witness?)

    C. There was no obstruction of Defendant's view of the stop sign.

    Evidence:
- i. Plaintiff's testimony
- ii. Police officer's testimony
- iii. Photographs of scene (Police? Newspaper? Witness?)
- iv. Witness Erin Dimmesdale's testimony

    D. State law imposes a duty on motorists to stop for stop signs and yield the right of way to motorists traveling on intersecting highways.

    Evidence:
- i. Citation to relevant law, e.g., 29-A M.R.S.A. Section

Once this step has been completed for each of the elements, we are in a position to develop an interview, investigation and discovery plan. Simply by reference to this analysis we can establish who we need to interview, e.g., the police officer and Erin Dimmesdale and about which topic inquiry must be made with each witness. We can also begin to list exhibits, which must be obtained through investigation or discovery, e.g., photographs of the scene, the police report or possibly Erin Dimmesdale's statement if one was taken.

Later, when investigation and discovery are complete, this same analysis provides the basis for compiling witness summary pages and exhibit lists.

Step 5: State the foundation needed to get the evidence admitted unless it is obvious.

Little is more devastating than being unable to enter otherwise admissible evidence at trial due to lack of proper foundation. Even if the attorney eventually establishes sufficient foundation, floundering to do so is embarrassing, to say the least, and so unnecessary. The foundation should be easily available to the attorney when the evidence is presented. For purposes of the next three steps it is best to set up a page in the notebook for each piece of evidence:

Prynne v Hawthorne

Cause of Action: Negligence

Elements of Negligence Cause of Action:

2. Defendant was subject to a duty

    Facts:
- A. There was a posted stop sign at the intersection of Main and High Streets on the date of the accident.

    Evidence:
- iii. Witness Erin Dimmesdale's testimony

Foundation: Personal Knowledge, Rule of Evidence 602
Witness has resided in next to the intersection since 1996. She sits on her front porch, about 75 feet from the stop sign, knitting most afternoons from 1 to 4 and was doing so on the date of the accident. She likes to watch the traffic and wave to neighbors as they drive by. She was watching as defendant approached and saw him go into the intersection. She had observed the sign before, during and after he entered the intersection. There was nothing obscuring her or the defendant's view.

With this information the attorney can easily establish the foundation for this evidence. Unless there is a valid objection, the evidence will be admitted. That brings us to the next step:

Step 6: State possible objections to the evidence.

This requires that your legal team switch roles and analyze the evidence from the other side—what objections would you make if you were trying to keep this out.

Prynne v Hawthorne

Cause of Action: Negligence

Elements of Negligence Cause of Action:

3.   Defendant was subject to a duty

   Facts:
   A.   There was a posted stop sign at the intersection of Main and High Streets on the date of the accident.

Evidence:
      iv.   Witness Erin Dimmesdale's testimony

Foundation: Personal Knowledge, Rule of Evidence 602
Witness has resided in next to the intersection since 1996. She sits on her front porch, about 75 feet from the stop sign, knitting most afternoons from 1 to 4 and was doing so on the date of the accident. She likes to watch the traffic and wave to neighbors as they drive by. She was watching as defendant approached and saw him go into the intersection. She had observed the sign before, during and after he entered the intersection. There was nothing obscuring her or the defendant's view.

Anticipated Objections:
Rule 601 (b) Disqualification of Witness: Erin is 93 and does not possess a reasonable ability to remember the matter. She spends her time knitting and waving because her aged mind cannot do more.

Having anticipated the objection, we can be prepared for it and have a response set out in the notebook in Step 7.

Step 7: State responses to possible objections with reference to the appropriate rule and pertinent case law.

Prynne v Hawthorne

Cause of Action: Negligence

Elements of Negligence Cause of Action:

2.   Defendant was subject to a duty

Facts:
A.   There was a posted stop sign at the intersection of Main and High Streets on the date of the accident.

Evidence:
iv.   Witness Erin Dimmesdale's testimony

Foundation: Personal Knowledge, Rule of Evidence 602
Witness has resided in next to the intersection since 1996. She sits on her front porch, about 75 feet from the stop sign, knitting most afternoons from 1 to 4 and was doing so on the date of the accident. She likes to watch the traffic and wave to neighbors as they drive by. She was watching as defendant approached and saw him go into the intersection. She had observed the sign before, during and after he entered the intersection. There was nothing obscuring her or the defendant's view.

Anticipated Objections:
Rule 601 (b) Disqualification of Witness: Erin is 93 and does not possess a reasonable ability to remember the matter. She spends her time knitting and waving because her aged mind cannot do more.

Response to Anticipated Objection 1:
The general rule is anyone offered is competent and the objecting party must prove incompetency. *Trial Handbook for Maine Lawyers,* Sec. 12.1. Capacity is at the discretion of the judge and can be determined through voir dire of the witness. *State v Brewer* 325 A2d 26 (1974, Me). The court can make inquiry itself. The courts generally resolve doubts in favor of competency and let the jury decide the weight to be given to the testimony. *Id.,* Sec 12.5.

We are almost done! All that's left is *Step 8: Cross reference your evidence to you Witness Summary Pages and Exhibit Pages.* We will look at the Witness and Exhibit List pages next. For now we'll just indicate here what is cross-referenced where:

Prynne v Hawthorne

Cause of Action: Negligence

Elements of Negligence Cause of Action:

2.   Defendant was subject to a duty

Facts:

A.   There was a posted stop sign at the intersection of Main and High Streets on the date of the accident.

Evidence:

iv.   Witness Erin Dimmesdale's testimony

Foundation: Personal Knowledge, Rule of Evidence 602

Witness has resided in next to the intersection since 1996. She sits on her front porch, about 75 feet from the stop sign, knitting most afternoons from 1 to 4 and was doing so on the date of the accident. She likes to watch the traffic and wave to neighbors as they drive by. She was watching as defendant approached and saw him go into the intersection. She had observed the sign before, during and after he entered the intersection. There was nothing obscuring her or the defendant's view.

Anticipated Objections.

Rule 601 (b) Disqualification of Witness: Erin is 93 and does not possess a reasonable ability to remember the matter. She spends her time knitting and waving because her aged mind cannot do more.

Response to Anticipated Objection 1.

The general rule is anyone offered is competent and the objecting party must prove incompetency. Trial Handbook for Maine Lawyers, Sec. 12.1. Capacity is at the discretion of the judge and can be determined through voir dire of the witness. State v Brewer 325 A2d 26 (1974, Me). The court can make inquiry itself. The courts generally resolve doubts in favor of competency and let the jury decide the weight to be given to the testimony. Id., Sec 12.5.

Cross References:

Witness—Erin Dimmesdale

Exhibits—Exh #10—Picture of intersection with stop sign

C. Exhibit Lists and Pages

Exhibit lists are important in and of themselves. The format of the exhibit list is often established by the rules of the court or jurisdiction in which your attorney practices. Often it provides spaces for the name of the exhibit, the date of the exhibit, the number of the exhibit, whether it was offered into evidence and whether it was admitted. This is quite useful to attorneys, judges and clerks for purposes of keeping track of exhibits at trial. However, the effective and empowered paralegal will go beyond the standard exhibit list.

A winning trial presentation needs more. Each exhibit must have its own page describing the exhibit and its place in the evidence schematic and must be cross referenced to the facts and witnesses to which it relates. Assume that a police officer took photographs at the scene of the accident in the *Prynne v Hawthorne* matter. Let's take a look at the exhibit page for the picture of the view of the stop sign as one approaches from the east. The basic information will include the same information as it appears on the exhibit list.

Plaintiff's Exhibit 10
Photo of approach to stop sign.
Date taken: June 4, 2006

This information is available to both sides and the court. However, it is not enough for us to effectively use the information (especially in cases with dozens of exhibits). We want to have that information available to us, but not to have it disclosed to the other side. We'll start with a basic description of the photo and its role in our case.

Plaintiff's Exhibit 10
Photo of approach to stop sign.
Date taken: June 4, 2006

Description:
Photo taken day of accident by police officer. Shows stop sign was in place and unobstructed view.

No exhibit can exist on its own. It will only be admitted if the criteria for admissibility are met—identification, foundation, relevance and so on. This is accomplished through one or more witnesses. All of this information should be immediately available to the attorney on Plaintiff's Exhibit 10's exhibit page.

Plaintiff's Exhibit 10
Photo of approach to stop sign.
Date taken: June 4, 2006

Description:
Photo taken day of accident by police officer. Shows stop sign was in place and the view was unobstructed.

Foundational witnesses:
Best: **Officer Thomas Jones**
    He took the photograph, can identify it, testify from what point it was taken and testify as to its accuracy as a representation of what it purports to represent
    Second: **Client**—can I.D. the subject of the photograph and testify as to its accuracy as a representation of what it purports to represent
    Third: **Erin Dimmesdale**—can I.D. the subject of the photograph and testify as to its accuracy as a representation of what it purports to represent

Testimonial witnesses:
Erin Dimmesdale—assist witness in explaining what she saw and her ability to see
Nathaniel Hawthorne—possible use to impeach

Now we're ready for the real meat of the exhibit page—how we actually get the exhibit into evidence and deal with possible objections. Fortunately this does not mean additional work. It is already done in the creation of the Evidence Tree. We simply copy that work here.

Plaintiff's Exhibit 10
Photo of approach to stop sign.
Date taken: June 4, 2006

Description:
Photo taken day of accident by police officer. Shows stop sign was in place and unobstructed view.

Foundational witnesses:
Best: **Officer Thomas Jones**
> He took the photograph, can identify it, testify from what point it was taken and testify as to its accuracy as a representation of what it purports to represent

Second: **Client**—can I.D. the subject of the photograph and testify as to its accuracy as a representation of what it purports to represent
Third: **Erin Dimmesdale**—can I.D. the subject of the photograph and testify as to its accuracy as a representation of what it purports to represent

Testimonial witnesses:
Erin Dimmesdale—assist witness in explaining what she saw and her ability to see
Nathaniel Hawthorne—possible use to impeach

Foundation
Rule 901(b): By way of illustration only, and not by way of limitation, the following are examples of authentication or identification conforming with the requirements of this rule:
(1) Testimony of witness with knowledge. Testimony that a matter is what it is claimed to be.

Foundational witnesses:
Best: **Officer Thomas Jones**
> He took the photograph, can identify it, testify from what point it was taken and testify as to its accuracy as a representation of what it purports to represent

Second: **Client**—can I.D. the subject of the photograph and testify as to its accuracy as a representation of what it purports to represent

Third: **Erin Dimmesdale**—can I.D. the subject of the photograph and testify as to its accuracy as a representation of what it purports to represent

Finally we'll tie this page back into the rest of the case through cross-references to the evidence tree and the witness pages.

Plaintiff's Exhibit 10
Photo of approach to stop sign.
Date taken: June 4, 2006

Description:
Photo taken day of accident by police officer. Shows stop sign was in place and unobstructed view.

Foundational witnesses:
Best: **Officer Thomas Jones**
He took the photograph, can identify it, testify from what point it was taken and testify as to its accuracy as a representation of what it purports to represent
Second: **Client**—can I.D. the subject of the photograph and testify as to its accuracy as a representation of what it purports to represent
Third: **Erin Dimmesdale**—can I.D. the subject of the photograph and testify as to its accuracy as a representation of what it purports to represent

Testimonial witnesses:
Erin Dimmesdale—assist witness in explaining what she saw and her ability to see
Nathaniel Hawthorne—possible use to impeach

Foundation
Rule 901(b): By way of illustration only, and not by way of limitation, the following are examples of authentication or identification conforming with the requirements of this rule:
(1) Testimony of witness with knowledge. Testimony that a matter is what it is claimed to be.

Possible Objections: If foundation is set, none anticipated. There is no aspect of the photograph that is prejudicial to the Defendant.

Response to Objections: N/A

Cross-references:
Evidence Tree:
Element 2. Defendant was subject to a duty
Fact A: There was a posted stop sign at the intersection of Main and High on the date of the accident
Fact B: There was no obstruction of Defendant's view of the stop sign

Witness Pages:
Officer Thomas Jones
Client
Erin Dimmesdale

D. Witness Lists and Pages

Like Exhibit Lists, the format for Witness Lists is often set by the court or the applicable rule of procedure. Some courts mandate forms. Like Exhibit Lists, Witness Lists themselves contain minimal information intended simply to put opposing parties and the court on notice. Thus, like Exhibit Lists, Witness Lists themselves are not extremely useful to the attorney conducting the trial. The effective and empowered paralegal will go beyond the standard witness list.

A winning trial presentation needs more. Each witness must have her own page providing the usual identifying information together with information about what evidence she can present, which exhibits will be used to assist her testimony and which exhibits she can identify. Again, we will want to include foundational information, possible objections to the witness or his testimony, replies to those objections and the like.

While most of the foregoing information is comparable to information on an exhibit page, there is one sort of information that should be included that does not have a counterpart on an exhibit page. We should include information regarding the witness himself other than simply identifying information. This type of information includes things such as:

- Whether a subpoena will be advisable or required, and, if so, where, when and by whom it should be served;
- Whether the witness needs any special accommodations, such as child care, transportation, sound amplification, wheel-chair access or a translator;
- Possible biases that might affect the witness's testimony, such as relationship to a party, an economic interest in the outcome or conviction of a crime that is admissible in court, especially if those biases are noticeable or discoverable by the opposition; and
- Special personality traits that might affect testimony or the presentation of testimony, such as stuttering, Turret's Syndrome, panic disorder, excessive nervousness or belligerence.

Much of the information contained on the witness page can be culled from other pages in the notebook. A typical witness page might look like this:

Prynne v Hawthorne: Witness Page
Erin Dimmesdale
   222 Accident Lane
   Boston, MA
   555-555-5555 Call before 10 a.m.
→ Requires transportation, hard of hearing.
Testimony relevant to: Cause of Action: Negligence, Element 1: Defendant
was subject to a duty
Facts: There was a posted stop sign at the intersection of Main and High Streets
on the date of the accident.

Foundation: Personal Knowledge, Rule of Evidence 602

Witness has resided in next to the intersection since 1996. She sits on her
front porch, about 75 feet from the stop sign, knitting most afternoons
from 1 to 4 and was doing so on the date of the accident. She likes to watch
the traffic and wave to neighbors as they drive by. She was watching as
defendant approached and saw him go into the intersection. She had
observed the sign before, during and after he entered the intersection.
There was nothing obscuring her or the defendant's view.

Anticipated Objection 1.

Rule 601 (b) Disqualification of Witness: Erin is 93 and does not possess
a reasonable ability to remember the matter. She spends her time knitting and waving because her aged mind cannot do more.

Response to Anticipated Objection 1.

The general rule is anyone offered is competent and the objecting party
must prove incompetency. *Trial Handbook for Maine Lawyers*, Sec. 12.1.
Capacity is at the discretion of the judge and can be determined through
voir dire of the witness. *State v Brewer* 325 A2d 26 (1974, Me). The court
can make inquiry itself. The courts generally resolve doubts in favor of competency and let the jury decide the weight to be given to the testimony.
Id., Sec 12.5.

Cross References:
   Exhibits—Exh. #10—Picture of intersection with stop sign
   Witness Statement given to police on date of accident

E. Witness Management

Many of the techniques for managing clients during litigation are applicable in a modified form to lay and expert witnesses. Unfortunately, a particular modification for a technique will seldom work for every witness; rather,
each witness will have a unique contribution and role in the process, and therefore will require a unique application of the technique. Nevertheless, there are

some generalities that can be established, and witnesses can, to a degree, be categorized for purposes of management.

While witnesses are part of the legal case and often very important to the presentation, they are not part of the legal team. However, they, like the client, must have an understanding of the nature of the presentation and their role in it, have an understanding of the court process and how it affects them, dress and act appropriately and be prepared. The extent of the understanding needed by each witness will depend on their contribution to the legal team's presentation.

Witnesses are not part of the legal team, because, unlike the client, they do not have a personal stake in the outcome, at least not in the same way as client does. No matter how much they want to help the client, their participation in the litigation imposes on them in a way it does not impose on the client. Their motivation is certainly different, and generally, they are less motivated than the client.

Even paid expert witnesses and relatives of the client will likely view themselves as doing the client a "favor." They expect to be accommodated and appreciated.

While the client may be effusive in her thanks, she lacks the legal professional's ability to accommodate the witness while simultaneously getting the witness's contribution as it is needed for a convincing presentation of the case. The attorney and paralegal also know the best form in which the witness's testimony can be obtained with the least inconvenience to the witness. In some cases, witness statements or expert reports will suffice. In others, depositions or trial testimony is necessary.

Categorizing Witnesses

Witnesses come in all forms—cooperative and uncooperative, rude and polite, education and uneducated, and so on. Your techniques for handling the witnesses must adapt to handling all types of personalities, understanding of the law and legal process, integrity and credibility. Such techniques are likely to depend on your personality and style, your attorney's personality and style, office policies and the like. Categorizing witnesses according to these factors may be helpful in developing particular techniques, but is not within the purview of this book.

Witness management can be separated into two basic components: preparation and accommodation (in the sense of getting what is needed from the witness while accommodating your presentation, the court's schedule and the witness's circumstances.) More helpful is categorization based on the importance of the witness to the case and their relationship to the client:

1. Witnesses who are important to the case and friendly to the client, e.g., a spouse who will testify as to the client's pain and suffering;
2. Witnesses who are incidental to the case and friendly to the client, e.g., an employer who will merely confirm the client was a good worker and lost wages;
3. Witnesses who are important to the case and neutral to the client, e.g., the witness to the color of the traffic light at the time of the accident;
4. Witnesses who are incidental to the case and neutral to the client, e.g., an ambulance attendant who will confirm the client's condition at the scene of the accident;
5. Witnesses who are important to the case and hostile to the client (not hostile in the sense that they are witnesses for the other party, but uncooperative or generally reluctant to becoming involved);
6. Witnesses who are incidental to the case and hostile to the client.

Generally the more important a witness is to a case, the greater the degree of understanding and preparation required; and the less friendly the witness is to the client, the more accommodation and "managing" is required. Proper witness management requires assessment of both of these factors.

In terms of importance, the spouse in the above example should be invited (and strongly encouraged) to engage in the same type of preparation as the client, i.e., an explanation of the causes of action, the theme or story of the presentation and their role in it, and the basics regarding evidence and proof; a tour of the court house; guidance on presentation and dress; review of likely testimony; and the like. An incidental witness need only understand what is expected of them, where it fits into the overall picture, and when/where they are needed (with small amounts of guidance regarding dress and presentation in some situations).

In terms of accommodation and management, the spouse is likely to require little—perhaps a subpoena to show her employer and, as always, instructions and reminders. He will likely accommodate himself to the scheduling needs of your presentation and be available at the courthouse throughout the proceeding. The "hostile" or uncooperative witness will require much more of management in this sense, including in some cases formal service of a subpoena by a process server and attorney preparation on the rules regarding having a witness treated as a hostile witness for purposes of direct examination. This, of course, will require monitoring of the whereabouts of the witness during the litigation and advance preparation so you are not "caught short" with too little time to find and serve the subpoena prior to deposition or trial.

General Practice Pointers for Witness Management

1. Know the court, the clerks and the manner in which they handle scheduling — are cases scheduled on a "trailing trial" list, will the court take witnesses out of order to accommodate witnesses especially expert witnesses, and is sequestration a standard procedure?
2. Keep the witnesses informed — when can they expect to give their statement, have their deposition taken, appear at court, how do they get to the court or deposition site, and what should they bring with them?
3. Keep informed regarding the witnesses — are they going on vacation, where do they work, do they need transportation, or do they have child-care concerns?
4. Make notes about, and report to your attorney, peculiarities about the witness — do they appear to be "tipsy" when you call after lunch time, do they express reluctance to be involved, do they seemed confused at times?

Conclusion — The Importance of Cross Referencing

A good trial notebook, like so much of what we do, requires analysis, thought, preparation and organization. The result of all that effort to accumulate comprehensive vital information in one spot can be overwhelming. As we saw with calendar and file management, simple accumulation of information is not enough.

In discussing file management we noted Nina Platt's formulation, "Case management = knowledge management = the creation of a system or process in an environment that allows all employees to have access to information they need to develop the knowledge to do their jobs." The trial notebook is such a system designed specifically to perform this function during a trial. I like to have a similar note book organized around the element-facts-evidence tree for each motion hearing, each deposition and the discovery process as a whole. Ultimately they evolve into and are cannibalized for the trial notebook.

As was true for the case file, the existence of the information in the file, even in an organized way, does not in itself provide the ease of access to the information needed to do the job. There must be a means of knowing where the information is and how to locate it quickly and accurately.

When it comes to the trial notebook, it is also necessary for the system to provide a map showing how each piece of information is connected to every other piece. It should illustrate how they are all connected to the ultimate goal of proving or disproving to the jury's satisfaction the elements of the causes of action that form the basis of the plaintiff's claims against the defendant. While we have spoken of this primarily in terms of civil actions, it applies in full force to criminal proceedings.

The key to providing "interconnectedness" information is cross-referencing. Each fact should be cross-referenced to the element(s) with which it is associated and the evidence which will be used to prove it. Each exhibit should be cross-referenced to the fact(s) and element(s) to which it relates, to the witnesses who will provide the foundation for its admission and the witnesses with whom it will be used. Each witness should be cross-referenced to the facts that will be shown by his testimony, the exhibits for which that witness will provide foundation and the exhibits that will be used to assist their testimony.

In the end, the well-designed trial notebook should allow even an attorney who has little familiarity with a case, working with the paralegal who put the notebook together, to try the case with a modicum of advanced notice. The notebook, combined with the paralegal's ability to manage time, workload, docket, file and the client in professional manner, provides the legal team with the tools needed for the perfect trial.

Conclusion

The Empowered Paralegal

Empowerment does not come from the outside. It comes from within. It is not granted, it is earned. The empowered paralegal gains that power and the confidence that comes with being a professional, competent, effective and efficient member of the legal team. In this book we examined some clear, concise and easy-to-use techniques for empowering paralegals. The essential skills were examined in detail, with management of time, workload, docket, files, clients and attorneys each being the focus of their own chapter. We then put all of that knowledge to work in the context of litigation.

Certainly the paralegal who can apply those techniques to effective management of their time, workload, docket, files, clients and attorneys will be a more effective, competent, efficient and professional paralegal. That paralegal will be, as a result, more empowered in her own eyes and those of her attorneys and clients. She will gain more respect and responsibility because she has earned more respect and responsibility.

Yet the point of this book is more than just explaining and transmission of practical techniques. The point lies in the basic underlying approach to all aspects of paralegal practices: the paralegal can manage each aspect rather than being managed by it. The paralegal can and must do so as the professional they are.

We focused on the management of specific aspects of paralegal practice, the ones that appeared to me, based on thirty years of practicing law, to be the most pervasive concerns of paralegals attempting to thrive in the American law office. Because most of my career has involved litigation, much of the discussion was cast in the context of the litigation paralegal. However, the principles underlying the techniques can, and should, be applied to every aspect of paralegal practice, in every type of office in which a paralegal works (law office, government office and corporate office), and in every area of law. My goal is that the paralegal who completes this book and applies these techniques will recognize in themselves the ability to manage their practice, gain self-confidence and the respect they deserve and feel the satisfaction and gratification of being a legal professional.

As we moved through each of the chapters dealing with management of time, workload, docket, files, clients and attorneys, we discussed particular techniques, but the underlying principles were the same in each. The techniques themselves are the result of applying those principles to whatever area in which the paralegal is seeking to become efficient, effective and empowered.

The first principle is to recognize and to account for the fundamental *inter*relationships and responsibilities of paralegal practice:

- The interrelationship between the facts, the file, the docket and time,
- The interrelationship between the client, the paralegal and the attorney, and
- The joint responsibility and involvement of all members of the legal team for the facts, the file and the docket in achieving a successful outcome.

The goal for the effective, empowered paralegal is to understand and to manage each of the key factors.

The second principle has to do with the way the paralegal approaches any and all aspects of paralegal practice. It is a proactive rather than reactive approach. It seeks to understand and manage even those aspects of practice that the paralegal cannot control. This principle involves taking a rational, empowered approach.

While the specifics varied in each of the chapters, in each chapter of this book we identified the areas of concern, analyzed each aspect of that concern, set priorities that addressed those concerns, sought a greater understanding of the area of concern, investigated solutions and barriers to those solution and established procedures for implementing solutions and removing or overcoming barriers to those solutions. We did so in a direct, rational and professional way. We did so in a way that honored our own need to be efficient, effective and empowered and honored the interrelationships and responsibilities of the first principle.

When a paralegal applies these principles, that paralegal finds empowerment through becoming efficient, effective and professional. Once empowered in this way, a paralegal is an essential member of the legal team in any office.

INDEX